The Silent Badge

STEVEN F. VERZAL
Retired Police Officer

PAGE PUBLISHING, INC.
New York, NY

First originally published by Page Publishing, Inc. 2019

ISBN 978-1-64350-632-6 (Paperback)
ISBN 978-1-64350-633-3 (Digital)

Printed in the United States of America

This book has been in the making for over thirty years. I have started it, stopped it, and started it again. After I found out that a close relative was thinking about going into the law enforcement field, I figured this was the right time to finish the damn book, so we start with the dedication.

This book and its contents are dedicated to all spouses and family members of police officers. They have to put up with the bull, the overtime, the pressures, and anything else that goes along with being married to a cop. If one marriage or family is saved or a proposal of marriage comes long after your career is established to see how this kind of life is actually lived because of this book, it was worth it.

Contents

The Whys and How Comes

S o you ask, Why did you write this book? Well, it sure wasn't for the money because some publishers will look at this and say, "This is stupid."

The real reasons I wrote this book were twofold:

1. People need to see what police go through. It isn't about race like today's news is talking about.
2. It's because prejudice starts at home. Yes, it does.

The following chapters will get into reason one, so we will leave that alone. But number two, get ready, I'm going to tell you some stuff that will curl your eyebrows.

I came from what I would *now* call a very prejudice family. I did not know it then because that was all I knew. There were words used like "nigger" and "coon," just to name a few. I heard this from parents, relatives, and so on. This started at home.

Just after graduating from high school, my mom and dad sat me and my 3 siblings down for a family discussion. They were getting a divorce. My siblings were all under 18, so the decision was that they would live with my mother. I, on the other hand, was 18 so I was to make my own decision about who I should live with. This decision was so difficult. I loved both of my parents so much and did not want to make a choice. At that time, the Vietnam Police Action was in full force, so I already had a draft number. Instead of siding with either of my parents, I told them that I should join the military since it was inevitable that I would be drafted. So, I joined. At that time, my father asked me, "Son what division are you going to join?" I told him that I would got to the recruiting office and take the first door to the right; that would be my destiny. On that day, I joined the US Army. My final destination was supposed to be South Korea. I was given 26 immunization shots to prepare me for my overseas assignment. However, after training across the various posts in the US to become an infantryman, my orders were suddenly changed, and I ended up in Anchorage Alaska. I don't think the typhoid shot was necessary for that assignment.

I reported in to my first sergeant, who was black (politically correct for that era), introduced myself, handed him my orders, and waited for him to say something. With his head down, he started to scan my papers. The Army is not afraid to use papers, lots and lots of papers. Did you ever hear the words "red tape"? You can thank the government for those two words.

My first shirt, nickname for a first sergeant, his head still down, flipping from page to page, finally looked up with an expression that could stop a train. "From Chicago, huh?"

"Yes, first sergeant," I replied.

"Come from a prejudice family?" he asked.

I hesitated for a second and thought to myself, *Why does he want to know that?*

Looking him straight in the eyes, as I'm getting ready to answer, he said, "We don't have prejudice in Alaska. If you are going to hate someone, hate them for who they are and *not* what they are. You may drive into a ditch some night, and the only three people to help you out are going to be black."

That was the best thing I had ever heard. I was still young enough that I wasn't set in my ways, and I could change my attitude. Now, as a much, much older man, I still believe in what he said. If you have to hate someone, hate them for who they are, not for what they are. And if you can, don't hate anyone.

This intro was not going to be in the book, but lately with all the police shootings, I believe there is a prejudice going both ways. There is no two-way respect. Before, if I told someone to stop, they stopped. Today, they run and then there are shots. The people must respect the police, and the police must respect the people. I'm telling you, this is a fact. If you grow up in a "white" neighborhood, chances are there will be some or even a lot of prejudice. The same goes for an African American neighborhood.

A few years ago, I was in the petting area of the zoo, and there were a bunch of children looking at some ducks in a pond. Then I saw and heard this little African American boy about six years old say, "Hey, Momma, look at the little nigger duck." Yes, prejudice starts at home.

I was in Chicago a few months ago, and on just one weekend, there were forty-two shootings. Yes, forty-two shootings, and not once did I hear about the race of the victim or suspects. So when African Americans shoot each other, that is okay?

In Milwaukee, CNN reported that there was a *black* teen shot by an African American police officer. Why the name change? The prejudice is there folks, and it has to stop. The time is starting to parallel the sixties; yes, I was around then. It has got to stop. Prejudice starts at home. Stop the prejudice first, and then the respect will come from both ways. If you teach your kids correctly, they will teach their kids correctly, and the cycle will continue. Do you see a pattern?

Many years ago in Florida, a patient with diabetes had the wrong leg cut off by his doctor. There was no mention of race. When a white man kills his white wife, there is no mention of race. When a white police officer shoots a white suspect, there is no mention of race. Why is that? See the pattern there?

When I was in the police academy, we were told: "There are no whites, blacks, or Eskimos here. You are all blue brothers." If we do not have prejudice on the force, why can't we do the same in society?

A few years ago, one of my siblings, whom I love to death, said to me, "You of all people should hate blacks. Look what he did to you." When people ask me, "What color was the guy that shot you?" My reply is, "I don't know. What color is an armed robber?"

So I have vented on the subject of police shootings; it is not an easy job. There are so many things you can do wrong in life to keep you from becoming a police officer. But if you were good, then the process starts as you will see in the upcoming chapters and the results that ensued after background checks, training, and finally, hitting the road on your own.

People have asked me, "Why did you become a cop?" Great question. I didn't have a death wish. I think I liked being a police officer because every day was different. When you got into your patrol vehicle, you had no idea what the day was going to bring until you saw it or they sent it to you—the fear or excitement of the unknown.

Chapter 1

The Predecision

The Silent Badge is twofold. A police officer *cannot* be silent in his or her personal relationship. He or she *must* communicate with his or her spouse. If the communication is not there, it is going to affect his or her performance while "on the streets." If an officer does not have 100 percent of mind and body on the street, he or she may have a "silent badge" forever.

The predecision of becoming a police officer will probably be the most important decision a person will ever make. The decision will be important to your mental stability. Sure, there will be decisions to make on the job, which will save your life, but the predecision will save your mind and possibly even others' lives.

I had to make the predecision twice: once to get out of the US Army infantry and go on to become a military police and a second time to get out of the US Army altogether and become a "real cop."

There is no comparison of being a military police to being a civilian police. The politics in the military are so lopsided that a private could do a minor thing, such as smoke marijuana, and get kicked out. You then have a master sergeant get drunk, almost kill a guy with a knife, and get convicted at his court martial, and they tell him to retire on a medical discharge. Justice? I do not think so.

That in itself, however, could be another book. We are here to discuss the decision to become a cop, whether civilian or military.

I had to make "the decision" twice, once when I was in the infantry learning to climb mountains, make igloos, and ski *up* a hill and learning how to walk on tundra and glaciers. The decision was easy for the wife: "I do not want you spending five days a week in the field, along with three weekends a month." The decision was made.

I really enjoyed learning all those things. I was having a blast, but I wasn't happy at home, so I checked out the possibility of changing jobs. I had above-average scores on all my entrance exams, so I could do just about anything the Army offered.

And by sheer coincidence, the MPs had come knocking on my door: "Your scores are great. How would you like to become an MP?" they asked. I then asked them how often I would have to go into the field with that job. "Two weeks twice a year." I took the offer, and it was there that my career as a police officer began.

Nothing had been brought up about how dangerous it was, rotating shifts, working holidays, etc. "You need to get out of the field," she said. I liked playing soldier in the field but had to keep her happy, so I agreed. Soon thereafter, she went home to Mama, I was an MP, and it was the best decision I had ever made.

I spent almost seven years in the Army, of which a little more than six years was as an MP. Big changes were happening: WAC (Woman's Army Corp) was disbanded, and women were moved into the barracks; we went from forty men bays to separate rooms (two men to a room), and I started to drink a lot and a lot more after that. The bars were open until 6:00 a.m. I would get back to my room, shower, and be on the job by 8:00 a.m., get off at 4:00 p.m., and go back to the bar. Then I met prospective wife number 2.

She was a bartender and waitress. We talked and then dated; I told her what I did. She said she wanted to get me out of the bars, so she proposed to me at dinner before I took her to work. All she cared about was keeping me out of the bars. There was never a discussion on long hours, overtime, the possibility of getting killed or wounded, or not ever seeing her or the family; it's just keeping me out of the bars. Great decision "I" made?

Like I said, being an army cop is nothing like being a *real* cop. There were more politics involved in decision-making than there was in the actual crime involved. The phrase "It's not who you know, but who you…" was an important phrase when a decision was made.

I took a squad of police officers to another military installation to help out due to a large group of twenty thousand or so troops that were in town to "play in the snow" or attend a field training exercise if you want to be politically correct. My squad doubled up with the other unit so we could run two-men cars. Well, my squad kept complaining to me that if a certain person working for a certain company was stopped for whatever, there was an apology for stopping them, and they were told to have a nice day.

The Alaska pipeline was being built, and the headquarters were at Fort Wainwright. There, the provost marshal, a major, was getting ready to get out and go work for the pipeline company. He did not want to ruffle anyone working for the pipeline's feathers, so his orders were as such: "If you stop anyone working for the pipeline, you will apologize for stopping them [even if it was for a DUI] and let them go without incident."

This did not sit well with me, so I went to see the major. He very nicely told me that when he retired, he was going to work for this company (they had offices on his military installation), and it was to his best interest to look the other way. When I said "no way," I was relieved of duty, sent back to my home unit, and was replaced. All this happened one month after I became a sergeant.

My company commander ripped me a new one, but my first sergeant just put his arm around me and said, "You took the bull by the horns and got stuck in the ass."

That is politics in the Army; need I say more?

Well, the time was coming for the city I was living in to begin booming due to the pipeline, and I do mean booming. MPs were getting out and going civilian, and my time in the Army was close to being up.

My best friend, Harry, had already gotten out and joined the Anchorage Police Department (APD) and told me that it was nothing like the military. I talked to my wife about becoming civilian police, and she did not care one way or another. She did, however, want to know how much they get paid.

One day, there was a knock at my door, and it was an APD recruiter. He had told me that Harry had told him I was getting "short," less than ninety days left in the service. We talked awhile about pay, training, etc., and then he left.

A couple of days later, I went to see the state troopers and asked the same questions. They could not guarantee where in the state I would be stationed after training, but there was a good chance it would be Anchorage.

Just when I thought I was ready to make my decision, the Army sent me orders to become an instructor at the MP Academy in Alabama. I was over six years, so my orders came on auto. If I wanted out, I had to go to Alabama for my last ninety days, get out, and fly back. What a waste. I went to see my first shirt, then the company commander, followed by the brigade commander, and finally, the post commander. I had appointments with three officers, and all they could say was that I was the backbone of the Army and I needed to stay in. The post commander finally gave in but said that if I came back in, I would have to sign a form, wait ninety-three days after discharge, come back in as a private, and start my career over again. I guess he tried to scare me into staying in. I asked where to sign.

The only predecision thinking that was made was from talking to troopers while on duty as an MP or when I walked foot patrol downtown with a city officer. They told me what life was really like on the streets, but my wife did not care. All she wanted was for me to sign with the highest bidder.

There needs to be a lot of discussion with a spouse or significant other. Just because you want to be a cop doesn't mean "I'm going to become a cop." The next few chapters are going to help you with the pre-decision-making process. Do not go out to dinner and just go to dinner. Talk, discuss, check it out, and then when you are done, talk, discuss, and check it out some more. One life is not at stake here. Yours, your spouse's, significant other's, and possible children's lives are all at stake here.

Chapter 2

The Decision

The *decision* had to be a good one. Which one paid the most? Which one was the most dangerous? With the state police, your backup might be fifty miles away. I liked their Smokey Bear hats and the $8,000 a year less than city. I like their Smokey Bear hats. The city had more people and was expanding faster than anyone could imagine: police academies every ten weeks and better chance of promotions. All the MPs going to civil law enforcement were going to the city. What a decision to make—$8,000 a year more than the state but no Smokey Bear hats.

I talked with my wife, and all she cared about was which one paid more. That was not going to be considered much in my decision-making process. Yeah, right. I was leaning toward the city, but I had to check out a few more things.

I contacted an old Army buddy who was once in the MP traffic unit. We had been friends for about three years while in the Army. One time, he investigated a traffic accident I was involved in where I flipped a police car attempting to avoid a moose. My platoon SGT tried to prove that I was driving too fast and that there was no moose. Harry showed with pictures and radio transmissions between the station and me that there was a moose in the roadway. I was called because it was in the commanding general's backyard. It was a priority call—politics.

STEVEN F. VERZAL

To this day, the only thing I remember was driving 30 mph in a 40 mph zone, a moose wanting to cross (not at a crosswalk), the brakes locking up, doing a couple of 360s, hitting a snowbank, and flipping the car. The next thing I knew was I was in the emergency room having x-rays. My body was one massive bruise. Witnesses in the hospital heard me repeating "Did I hit the fucking moose?" I was told no.

Another time, I was attempting to find an injured moose that had crawled away from a traffic accident. I was driving slowly in the woods because I knew there was a small lake nearby. Well, the front left side of the vehicle found the water. What I mean is, it broke the ice and then found the water. Harry was the one who called the tow truck.

Harry was the guy I could talk to, and he would give me the poop on the police department. Harry, his wife, my wife, and I hung out together often. We bowled, went to dinner, and were just altogether great friends. When we talked about the change from military to civilian police, he said there was no comparison. I would not have to put up with the politics that I dealt with in the Army and, once I was off probation, I would really love it. Harry got out of the Army about a year before my tour was up and was already off probation on the city department when I had finally thought about joining.

That was the nice thing about the huge city expansion; as one got out of the military, he was a personal reference for the next guy and so on. Harry was my reference. He talked to me about permanent shifts after training was over. I would no longer have to rotate shifts every thirty days like I did in the Army.

While in training, I would work two weeks on shift A, four weeks on shift B, and four weeks on shift C and then spend my final two weeks back on shift A. We talked about how there was always a backup unit available because of the city's rapid expansion. A backup unit was called when a one-man car felt that something wasn't quite right in a situation. We talked about training, polygraph tests, oral board, and, of course, salary. Midshift was paid 4 percent more than first shift; late shift got 8 percent more; and if I finished college, which the city paid for, I would earn even more.

While my wife may have had her questions answered about the salary, I still had some questions for Harry. He told me not to worry that there were no politics and the work was about the same.

Harry could not have been more wrong. I do not know if he just overlooked things that he thought I already knew or he just assumed that I knew them. I was going to find out a lot more than I was told, like unions (they actually were politics), the blue flu, and many other things that will be discussed later.

I guess the best way to make your decision is for your spouse to talk to other spouses for their experiences. First, if you can, find out if that couple is happily married. If they are, their answers will be given without prejudice. Next, see if the department has a reserve or ride-along program. You will not get paid, but you will have a good idea of what goes on in the department. If you can, try out different shifts. You may go on a day shift ride-along and say, "Wow, this is easy." Then you may join the department, get put on the midshift (swings), and think that it's completely different from what you originally saw.

Check it out from the top to the bottom. Do not go in with a lot of questions. Try to get the answers *before* you sign on the dotted line. Talk to the chief. Most large departments have a recruiting department—talk to them. Nine out of ten times, they, too, were on the streets at one time. They will be straight with you. They do not want to hire someone that is going to be a handicap to themselves or others.

Last, if you are not sure, if you have questions, or your spouse / significant other has questions, *wait*! Do not jump in until you are ready. Hold off on the decision.

My father, a very wise man, once said to me: "What awaits you will never miss you."

Chapter 3

The Process

N ow that the decision is made, we move on to the process. I call it the process because it could be a long, long process. Depending on the department, the process may be quick if they are hiring now; or if they are not, pack your lunch because it could be a while.

Depending on the department, there may or may not be an order for the processing of an application. It could go: application, wait for background check, written test, polygraph, oral board, and then wait until an opening. In my case, the department was hiring so many officers. There was not any order on how things progressed. It was the luck of the draw.

Step one in the process is to fill out an application. Again, depending on the department, it could be long or short. The department that I applied for was fourteen pages. Yes, it was fourteen pages. They are going to ask you everything from gambling to your sex life, personal life, family life, and work history, whatever they want. Be honest, very honest. Why? You will find out later.

I was asked questions on gambling. Do you gamble? With what? Cards, sports, slot machines, pinball machines? And yes, pinball machines are a form of gambling. You put in money, and you are gambling to win a free game.

Sex life was the next one that was very interesting. Have you had any form of weird sex? What a question to ask. What is weird sex? That will be discussed later.

Personal life was not so bad: single, married, how many kids, divorced, parents, dead, or alive. How many times have you been married? If more than once, did you get a divorce before you married again? Where were you married, divorced, or remarried? Why do they want to know this? Later, I say.

What kind of drugs do you take? Aspirin is a drug; do not forget. Have you taken any illegal or recreational drugs? How much did you take and when? Are you still taking them? Do you know anyone that takes illegal/recreational drugs? Be honest; it is important. Again, you will find out later.

Have you ever been arrested? That was a good one. How long ago? Were you under seventeen years old? Were your records sealed? What type of a crime was it? Was the crime you committed a felony or a misdemeanor? A felony is defined as punishment where a person can be confined to jail or prison for more than one year. With a misdemeanor, the punishment is less than one year.

This is the gist of the application. It is very, very, very important that the questions are answered as honestly as possible. The reason why would be discussed later.

The application is done; your background check is still pending. Now, it is time for the written test. The test is usually numerous parts, which could include, but not limited to, math, English, and comparisons, and the last part is situations. The situation part will be explained in a minute.

You see, the department does not want to hire idiots, so the test has got to have basic questions about the three Rs. If I have to explain to you what the three Rs are (readin', 'riting, and 'rithmetic), then I don't believe you are police material. Here comes the fun part of the test: the situation part.

The situation part is a commonsense part. I will say it again: a *common sense* part. This is the part where you are in a situation and you have to make a decision. *You must make a decision.* The situation I liked best was you get called to a house where a mom says her twelve-year-old boy has locked himself in the bathroom and will not come out. What do you do? (A) Kick the door in and bring him out; (B) tell the mom there is nothing you can do and leave; (C) attempt to talk the boy out; (D) you are not qualified to do this, so call in an expert, such as a family counselor or child psychologist. The answer will not be given. All the situation questions are like that. What would a normal John Doe citizen do if he was in that type of situation?

Common sense, common sense, common sense. Need I say more on the subject?

Okay, I know I should not say this, but we will assume you passed the test. I got a ninety-eight on mine, by the way. The next step is the polygraph or lie detector as some people call it. The Supreme Court of the land says you cannot use the results of a polygraph in court, but you *can* use them for the hiring of different occupations. And guess what, law enforcement is one of them.

What can I say about the polygraph? Well, for one, you cannot beat it. Many people have tried; it does not work. If you are not going to be honest, be something else, not a police officer. I think one of the questions should be "Do you think you are prejudice, or, are you prejudice?"

Remember a few lines back when I discussed the fourteen-page application? Well, some departments use that fourteen-page questionnaire as a guideline for checking your honesty. This is the main goal of the polygraph.

Now, that does not mean "Yes, I killed someone" means that you are honest. What they want to know is, (a) Did you do drugs as a kid? (b) And did you tell the truth about it? One question that really got me was, Have you ever had kinky sex? Well, I stayed silent for a while and looked at the examiner, and he said to me, "If it happened in the bedroom, it is not considered kinky. It means with animals, etc." I immediately said no. Well, approximately an hour later, the test was over. The examiner said I could go and I would be notified of the results. I asked if I passed. He then said, "What do you think?" I said I passed. He then advised me that "off the record" (a phrase you will use a lot), I passed.

It was now two down and one to go with one pending (the background check). The oral board was next.

A few days later, I reported to the oral board. I walked into an office; seated there was a captain, a sergeant, a corporal, and three patrolmen. I sat down feeling like I was the center of attention, and I was. I just sat there and answered questions that were thrown at me. "Why do you want to be a cop—and upholding the law could not be the answer?" Well, that was easy.

I wanted to be a city officer because it paid more (wife). They said I was honest.

The oral board is there: one, to see who you are and two, to see how you would answer questions about life in general. My favorite was, Can you work for a female corporal/sergeant? I thought to myself that was a good question. I thought about it for a minute and said, "Sir, I have been in the Army for almost seven years, and the only way I can answer that is to use my experience in the Army." The captain said, "Okay, answer it." I said, "Sir, the only experience I have working with women as police officers was that, in my opinion, the only two reasons women joined the Army was [a] to find a guy and get married and [b] because they were gay." They asked me a few more questions, and I was done. They asked me if I had any questions, and I said no. I was advised I would be notified in a week or so.

After I was hired on, I worked with one of the patrol officers who was on my board. He told me that after I left the room, they discussed my answers. He said the one about the women in the Army made the captain laugh. He said that that was the only time he saw the captain laugh during the tenure of the oral boards.

A week or so later, I was notified via US mail that I had been accepted to the police academy that was starting in four weeks. I was really happy, I think.

Chapter 4

The Academy

Congratulations if you have made it this far. You are about one-third of the way there. The academy is where the brain and the body go on overdrive. Be prepared for anything, and I do mean anything.

I could probably write a book just on the academy, but I will keep it to just one chapter. Some things that I feel are important I will dwell on; other things, I may skip them or omit them altogether. There has to be some things you have to find out on your own.

The academy is going to test the mental and physical limits of the body and brain. You are going to go through physical training, self-defense, pursuit driving, and firearms training; then the brain is going to have to remember city law, state law, and some federal law; you will be taught observation techniques, apprehension, radio talk, and phonetic alphabet, and when you are done, put it on a paper. Then when the paperwork is done, be prepared for court time. While you are learning all this, there may be daily, weekly, midterm, and, of course, the final test.

I just explained a nine- to twelve-week academy in one paragraph, but it will not be that easy. When you get home at night, if it's not a live-in academy, you may be tired; you will be drained from the day, and you might even have homework. Sounds fun, doesn't it?

The very first instructor introduced himself and said, "Let's start off with prejudice." There is no prejudice in the police department. Well, there shouldn't be (i.e., Rodney King). You are all brothers and sisters, and there is no race in the department. You are all *blue* brothers and sisters (our uniforms were all blue then). If you hate a race, drop it and forget about it. If you are white and your backup partner is black, so what. Get used to it. Remember, you are all *blue*.

Usually, the chief or his representative gives a speech about how nice it is to see everyone. Take it with a grain of salt; they will can you in an instant. *Do not* let your guard down ever. Again, do not let your guard down ever.

You are here to learn the law and to enforce it. I say again, you are here to learn the law and to enforce it. You do not interpret the law. That is for the courts to do. You do not make the laws, the legislature does. This is why we have different levels or branches of government. I remember being told "Every week, the laws change." Why? Because when the Supreme Court makes a ruling, that ruling may change the law.

Garbage was a good example. Before a USSC (United States Supreme Court) ruling, a search warrant was needed to go through a person's garbage. For example, a guy was running a bookie operation, and there were a lot of pieces of paper in his garbage in the alley. The police checked it without a warrant, and he was convicted. It was determined that a search warrant was needed to go through his garbage, and the conviction was appealed. The USSC said that once it is in the alley in a garbage, anyone can go through it; no search warrant is needed. The conviction was upheld.

There have been many times over the course of history when the USSC has stepped in to modify the law because of unusual circumstances. Ever wondered why you see cops read a guy his rights? Back in the sixties, a guy by the name of Miranda was stopped in Arizona. He wanted an attorney, and things took far too long for the police to do anything. So he was convicted of his crime. His attorney then took it to the USSC to argue that his client wanted an attorney after he was arrested, and now there is a Miranda warning: you have the right to remain silent, the right to an attorney.

The laws of the land (city, state) and some federal will not be touched on. I will say just prepare your brain to be filled to its capacity.

You want to be in good physical shape for the agility test. There are different tests for each department, so be prepared to do just about anything. We had to run up a few flights of stairs, kick a door in, grab a 150-pound mannequin, and then carry it down the stairs to safety within a certain time limit.

You will be taught self-defense tactics, but just enough to get you by. You will not be a Bruce Lee when you are done. In fact, that reminds me of a story, but I will bring it up later. You are taught some really cool holds using leverage, but you are told they may not work if the person outweighs you. You could then use your nightstick. You will have intense training on this and where to hit the person, not in the head. The collarbone is a good place or even the solar plexus. To use your gun, you better be in fear of your life or protecting someone else's life. Some of the police today are shooting ten or twelve rounds and not hitting anything or hitting the suspect once; we had six shot revolvers and were told if you can't hit him or her with the first five, put the sixth one in your own head (ha ha).

Firearms training was fun for me. We used the FBI combat course, which starts you at three feet and you go all the way to fifteen yards. Get really good with your sidearm. We had to qualify once a quarter with fifty rounds. I fired fifty rounds a month plus qualified every quarter. I never did worse than expert. When I was done, there was a big hole in the bull's-eye. My expert shooting would come in handy someday.

Pursuit training was also a blast. They took us to a remote runway at the airport in the winter time and hosed it down (thanks to the fire department), and because of the cold weather, the water became ice in minutes. They told us they were going to teach us how to safely drive fast and safely stop. Boy, were they right. Always keep control of your patrol vehicle. The life you save may be your own or not.

They set up these cones, and half of the class drove while the other half kept putting the cones back. They were really getting scattered. When the class was over, we were good, not great, but good.

Get keen on your observation technique. Do not get good at it; get great at it. You will be a trained observer. You will see things that are not ordinary to the average John Doe citizen. When you see things that are not quite right, you will get nosy. This is what you are paid to do.

We were talking about observation techniques when the back door of the classroom crashed open. A guy ran up with a gun in his hand, screamed "You've been fucking my wife!" at the instructor, and fired the gun numerous times, and the instructor went down. He then turned and ran out of the classroom. In the panic, we hit the floor, and there was a lot of commotion. Then the instructor got off the floor and said, "Take out a piece of paper. What did you see and hear, what kind of gun, what did the person look like, and how many shots were fired?" When we were done, there were thirty-one different descriptions of what had happened. The "bad guy" came back in (he was a cop), and boy, were we all pretty wrong. Later, I will give examples of the average citizen and their observations.

The course on writing traffic tickets was also fun. There was a lot of debate on "quotas." Our policy was "We have no quotas. You can write as many tickets as you want." There was a discussion on speeding and how fast over the limit they have to be before you can stop them. A big item that was pushed was "officer discretion." It is up to the officer to make the final decision on whether a citation should be issued. We had to notify dispatch after the traffic stop was over on whether it was a ticket or a warning given.

The class on dead bodies / crime scene was also very interesting. You see, back when there was no CSI (crime scene investigator), we did it all: dusted for prints, pictures, etc. Then the detectives showed up, and the case was turned over to them.

We had a crime scene that we had to do all the prelim work on and then write a report. It was really cool; we were split up into teams and had to investigate this crime scene with a dead body. Well, no one knew who the person was, no ID. But as it turned out, the license was under the victim. The only team that found it was my team. It seems that people, even cops, have a problem with touching dead bodies. This class was given to break people of that phobia. The only reason I knew to check under the body was because I had a couple of dead body calls when I was in the military. You have to investigate thoroughly when at a crime scene.

You will also find out in the academy who the "smart ones" are. Just because a person is smart does not make them a good officer. We started with almost thirty-seven or thirty-eight cadets on day 1, and I think thirty-one graduated. We had all races, both sexes, and a few weird ones (they didn't make the final cut). After you graduate, you will still lose a few "rookies." It is not an easy job.

Well, I do not want to get off topic; it is easy to do, so back to training at the academy.

When we went to our first, and only, autopsy, I must admit it was incredibly fascinating. We had a gentleman who had been shot at close range with a large-caliber handgun. The bullet entered his left nostril but did not exit. We were to watch Doc Rogers, our ME (medical examiner) find a cause of death.

The class formed a circle around the table and watched as the autopsy began. Without being too gruesome, I will explain what I observed. First, a "Y" was cut into his chest, and the skin was pulled back. The ribs were cut with a saw so the ME could get to the vital organs: heart, lungs, etc. He took out the heart and said it was in good shape. He then took out a lung and showed us these little black dots; the dots were proof that the person was a smoker. The ME then cut the back of the victim's neck and pulled the skin up over his face revealing the naked skull. The face was like a mask; it was really cool. He then took out a round saw and cut off the top of the skull, revealing the brain. I was so intrigued by this that I was sort of crowding the ME. He looked at me and said, "Do you want to give me a little room?" I backed off a little, allowing him to finish his examination. He took the brain out, dug on it a little, and pulled out the bullet, a .357 mag. That was the cause of death. I looked at the brain that was in a bowl and made a comment that it looked like spaghetti. Three students ran out of the room. My instructor made a comment about being professional. I had no further comments about the autopsy. When you go to an autopsy, learn to breathe through your mouth. The mouth cannot sense smells, which is usually what gets you sick.

If it is blood that makes you sick, learn to live with it or find a different career. Some days, it may be like working in an emergency room.

There were many discussion forums during the academy. One that really interested me was the department being represented by a union. It seems that the police officers were in a union (Teamsters), but the corporals, sergeants, and high-ranking officers (i.e., lieutenants, captains, etc.) were not. Then my question was, Were unions really necessary for the well-being of the department? Well, the discussion never really went anywhere, so I let it die for the time being until finals.

As the academy was getting closer to graduation, the talks became more in-depth on certain subjects. The FBI came in and taught us a class on how to approach a suspicious person. This is going to be important later in the book.

As we were getting closer to the end of the academy, we watched a movie and were told about a book. The book was called *Officer Down, Code Three*.[1] It was the best book I had ever read. It is about the deadly errors that a police officer makes that can get him killed. Some of the examples were not keeping your firearm in working order, sleeping on duty, apathy, and so on. The book was written in the mid-1970s, but it is still relevant today and should be in every cop's library.

We were now getting down to the final weeks, and we had to pick a subject for an essay that would be part of our final grade. I had problems with picking a subject, and then *bam*, it hit me: police unions, for or against, would be my topic. My instructor agreed. I came up with fifty questions and sent them to one hundred departments (two in each state, one to a small town under ten thousand people and one to a city with over one hundred thousand people). I sent the questions with a cover letter and a self-addressed return envelope. I got fifty back, of which twenty refused to answer the questions, so I did my survey on the remaining thirty cities.

The results I came up with were not astonishing. If you are from a little "Mayberry" town, you do not need a union because you

---

[1] Pierce R. Brooks, *Officer Down, Code Three*.

just go to the chief who would then go to the city council to get what you want. If you are a large department, you need a union, if for no other reason but bargaining. The rest of the final went well. I got a very good passing score. There was also some hands-on testing. Nine and one-half weeks after reporting to the academy, I had passed. I was no longer a cadet. I was now a rookie.

Chapter 5

The Probation

It was time to hit the streets. The probation period where I came from was more or less split into two parts. The first part was with an FTO (field training officer). The on-the-street training was a minimum of twelve weeks: two weeks on day shift with one FTO, four weeks on swing shift, four weeks on graveyard, and then the final two weeks back on days. On those final two weeks, you were on your own, making decisions; and hopefully, your FTO was not too far away in an unmarked if you needed him. Because of my prior MP background, I really was not worried, but I knew he was there somewhere, at least I hoped.

To be an FTO required extra training, and the officer had to have a few years on the force. The FTO had to fill out a daily, weekly, and monthly paperwork on the rookie and then get together with the other two FTOs, and they had to determine if the rookie was ready for the street or if more training was needed.

My first FTO was Joe, and he made quite the impression on me: a really good impression. He was the public relations officer for the department and went back on the street when the city expanded. The city went from a few service areas to many areas; then you had to figure in traffic units for accident investigation and radar and throw in a few backup units, and each shift also had at least one corporal, sergeant, and lieutenant.

My first shift was the day shift. The shift was 8:00 a.m.–6:00 p.m. All shifts were ten hours each, overlapping with the previous shift by two hours. This way, if we were not busy, the last two hours were used to finish up any paperwork that had not been completed during the time on the street.

Joe had asked me where in the city I wanted to work, and I told him that I didn't care. When it was time to choose an area, we chose downtown. The area was one of the smaller areas, but it covered the center of the city.

He showed me which corners the "ladies" hung out. We also went by a few bars that were visited by these "ladies." I think if I just say "ladies," you will know what I mean, unless "hookers" is a better word. Joe also liked to drive by the courthouse and watch the women go to lunch. It was summer, and the skirts were short. He did all the driving the first day, and all we did was talk. He explained how I needed to learn the streets and know where I was at all times. He said, "If you do not know where you are, how can you call for backup?"

We spent about half of the shift walking the downtown area. We hit all the bars that were hangouts for the locals. We would walk behind the bars and would find drunks sleeping it off. I think Joe felt okay with me because of my previous experience. We made a few traffic stops; he talked the first time, and then I did the rest. On my first one, with Joe observing, we watched a guy roll through a stop sign. We discussed in advance if it was going to be a warning. When I came back to the patrol car to check for warrants, I asked Joe if I should say anything to the driver. He said to tell him that he wasn't in California. I went back to the driver, handed him his license and registration, and stated, "I am only giving you a warning this time. Just remember, you aren't in California." I walked back to the car, and Joe was laughing. I asked him why he was laughing at me, and he said it was because he didn't think I would say anything about California to the driver. I said, "You are my FTO. I do what you tell me to do."

The rest of the first two weeks went as planned with no major foul-ups. I do remember the first call I went on, and it was pretty amusing. We got a call to a disturbance at a bar right across the street from the police station. I went in, Joe told me to handle it, and he stood back for me to be the officer in charge. I found this older couple in their sixties who had called the police. I was talking to the husband about what had happened. He told me that he and his wife just flew into town, wanted to have a drink, and thought it was a good safe place to have a drink being across from the police station. They sat down and the waiter came over and took their order, but when he came back with their drink, he made a pass at him. I said, "You mean he made a pass at your wife?" He repeated no that the waiter made a pass at him. I said, "What did you do?" He said, "I got up and cold-cocked him." I looked at Joe in the corner, just laughing his butt off.

I then went up to the bartender and asked him if he saw anything. Now, this guy was about six feet, eight inches and weighed about 290 pounds. When he started to talk, his voice was so high it almost broke my glasses. He told me exactly what the patron had said. I looked back at Joe, and he was still laughing uncontrollably. I went over to Joe to confer, and we came to a conclusion. I then went to the victim and asked him if he wanted to press charges. He said that he did not. I went to the couple and gave them the address of another bar that they could walk to and have a quiet drink in that was not a gay bar. Joe knew that it was a gay bar, and I didn't, and he did not tell me. That's why it was so funny to him.

At the end of my two weeks, Joe told me that I did very well and that he was looking forward to seeing me for my final test: the last two weeks.

Swing shift was from 4:00 p.m. to 2:00 a.m. It was a lot busier than day shift. Due to the vacation schedule, I had two different FTOs. One of my FTOs was the instructor for pursuit driving in the academy. When he drove, he drove well. Swing shift was filled with a lot of domestics. Those are when the husband and wife have a problem and fight, and then someone calls the police. Usually, the drink of choice was some type of alcohol intoxicant. You see, alcohol on its own merit does not have an odor. So you cannot say that you smell alcohol; you say that you smelled an alcohol intoxicant. I know it sounds picky, but that is the way it is done.

When I was on days, I came home while my wife and daughter were still awake; but with swings, it was totally different. I would get home at around 3:00 a.m., and everyone was asleep. There was no one to say, "Hi, honey, how was your day?" Some days, I would get home and just sit in the living room for an hour or two, going over things that I had done and contemplating if they were right or wrong decisions.

I remember one swing shift, I was driving and my FTO told me to make multiple turns in a row. We then drove through an alley, and he screamed, "I've been shot! Where are we?" I had no idea where we were.

He said it was very important to know where you are at all times. Joe told me that on days, and I had forgotten it. I never forgot it again. This was the second and last time I was told to know where I was at all times. That discussion was never brought up again. From then on, no matter who was driving or what shift it was, I always watched street signs, and I *always* knew where I was.

I think though that swing shift was pretty slow in general. There was not a lot to talk about. I saw Joe one day when he had a rookie on swings. He asked me how things were going, and I said fine. I told him I thought swings would be busier. He said that an average cop, in twenty years, may never pull his gun once, let alone shoot it. I said thanks; I guess I was just expecting a little more.

There was one high-speed chase. We were chasing a Corvette that blew a red light, and boy, was he flying. He had a faster car, but due to my pursuit training, I knew that you make up for speed as you go around corners while you prevent fishtailing. I was closing in on him around corners because he was fishtailing and I wasn't. This is where you catch up. I was driving and I did fairly well except on one turn, I did not keep both hands on the wheel, and my FTO (who had taught the driving class) slapped my hand and said, "Always keep both hands on the steering wheel!" One time was all it took. He finally pulled over when he saw a police officer coming toward him. I chalked up one arrest—speeding, eluding a police officer, reckless driving (oh yeah), and a tow truck bill.

With the exception of the street sign thing, I had no problems on swing shift. At the end of the four weeks, I was going to midnights.

The dreaded midnight shift is the divorce maker. You go to work while your family sleeps. You come home, your family is awake, and you go to sleep. Sounds like fun, right? I think the guys liked midnights because it paid more. Most of the fights were at bars, and the bars were winding down. The bars were open until 6:00 a.m., but if it was not a Friday or Saturday night, things were pretty quiet.

The shift went from midnight until 10:00 a.m. It was the first time I got to see Harry for any length of time. He loved the late shift. But Harry had changed. I was not sure how, but he was not the same Harry from the Army. He had about a year more on the force than I did, but he had changed. Later, I would find out why.

The midnight shift was so boring; I cannot remember my FTO's name or anything that happened on that shift. That is pretty bad, or maybe, it was just boring. Or maybe it was a combination of both.

By this point, I had finished ten weeks of training with an FTO. It was now time for the final test: two weeks on my own, with Joe following me (I thought and hoped).

I went to day shift, and there was no Joe. I asked around to see where Joe was. They told me that he was running late, and I should wait for him. When it came to my area, I asked for downtown and got it with no problem. Just before we hit the streets, in walked Joe in civilian clothes. I asked him what he was doing, and he told me that he had to get an unmarked squad to follow me. That's right; I was on my own. Here came the final two weeks.

I think that if I hadn't had the MP background, I probably would've had more supervision during the last two weeks. But that was okay with me. Joe asked me what area I took, and I told him downtown (area 2). He said okay, go do it and that he would be around if I needed him.

Things were fairly quiet; I kept looking over my shoulder for Joe, but I never saw him. But when I would make a decision, I would hear on the radio "good call." I would look around, but I wouldn't see him. Then I would go on another call, and I would hear him laugh on the radio. I could not find him, but I knew he was there. This went on for the first week. I would see him before the shift and then not again until after the shift. I guessed I was doing okay because if I wasn't, he would be there.

I do remember one call where there was a report of someone breaking into a vacant building. I got there and another rookie arrived as my backup. Since I was the first one on the scene, I was in charge. We drew our firearms out of our holsters and entered the building. No one could be found, the owner was called, the building got locked, and we started talking out in front of the building. The rookie, whom I do not remember his name but he was in the academy with me, made a comment that while drawing my pistol, I pointed it at him and that I shouldn't have done that. I told him that he was mistaken and that with my years of MP training and experience, I knew all about firearms safety. He disagreed with me. While he was one of the smartest cadets in the class, he washed out and didn't make it through the FTO phase. He was given a chance for additional training, but he refused and then resigned. Just because you are smart doesn't necessarily mean you will be a smart police officer.

Well, at the end of the second to the last week of FTO training, Joe sat down with me and asked me if I had any questions. I told him that I didn't and asked why. He told me that we had an appointment with the captain. Now, this was the guy that I made the comment about women to while interviewing with the oral board. We went up to see the captain, and he asked me how I was doing. I said I was fine, wondering why he was asking and why I had been called up by him. The captain said he had looked over all the paperwork from my FTOs and that they had decided to waive my last week and put me on the streets a whole week early. I asked why, and the captain said, "Do you think you are ready?" I told him that yes, I was ready. The captain told me that my FTOs also thought I was ready. The meeting was over. He said congratulations. Joe and I left, and while we were walking to the squad room, he said, "Don't let me down." I told him I wouldn't and that he would be proud of me.

That was the official end of my FTO program. I still had nine more months of probation, but I was now on my own. They asked me what shift I wanted to work, and I told them days. I would have the next three days off and then begin working four tens (four days a week, ten hours each shift). Since I was a rookie, I had to take the days they gave me to work: Friday, Saturday, Sunday, and Monday. There was no problem. My wife did not care.

Chapter 6

Out on Your Own / Not at Home

M ost of the patrol duties were day-to-day tasks. I averaged about two hundred to three hundred miles driven on a shift. Now that I was on my own, and really didn't have anyone looking over my shoulder, I really felt comfortable. Some of the cases that I got involved in, which I believe are important, will be brought up in later chapters. I was also working five to six days a week due to a shortage of officers; therefore, I was not at home very often.

This chapter is going to be based more on the everyday calls that an officer runs into, such as traffic accidents, running radar, coffee breaks, bank robberies, lunch, some foot patrol, stopping for donuts, and of course, paperwork.

We had a policy of not giving a ticket unless the speeder was doing at least 10 mph over. The reason for this was to take into consideration an older car because as it got older, the speedometer cable would stretch and the speed shown would not be accurate. Well, I made a slight change to that; my rule was thirteen over. Why thirteen? Because that's an unlucky number that would add more to their unlucky day. If they were speeding in a school zone, it was 4 mph over because I felt as if it was my job to protect the little kids from the big cars.

I was running radar one day, and a yellow Corvette went flying by doing 70 mph in a 55 mph zone. I pulled the car over, and this very good-looking female was driving. I asked for her license and registration, and she complied. I went to the front of the vehicle to check the VIN number on the dashboard against the registration. While looking at the VIN number, I noticed that the driver started to pull her already short skirt up even higher than it was meant to be, smiling at me while doing it. I went back to my vehicle; she had no outstanding warrants, so I filled out a ticket. I walked back to her vehicle, handed her back her ID, and then handed her a ticket. She said, "Didn't you see what I was showing you?" I said, "Yes, I did. Nice pink panties. Have a nice day."

People would do all kinds of things to get out of a ticket. So I came up with another of my own policies: if the excuse was one that I had never heard before, I gave them a warning (as long as they were not going too fast). So the first I'm late for work, late for church, etc., they got off. But the second time I heard it, forget it. It did not work.

I was running radar one Sunday morning, and I clocked a car doing 13 mph over. I pulled him over and asked for the usual stuff. He looked at me and said, "Officer, I am really sorry. I am a Bishop. I am the highest-ranking LDS Mormon in the state, and I am late for church. I have 250 people waiting for me." Well, I thought to myself, *You don't mess with God's people on Sunday.* So I told him to slow down. He said he would never speed again. Off he went and end of story, right? No, it was the beginning of the story. I get back to the squad room at the end of the shift, and I am working on paperwork. The corporal and sergeant were looking over the tickets issued by the shift when they looked at me and said, "Officer, will you stand up?" I asked what I did. The corporal then told me that his wife was in church that day, and the minister was late. He had come running into the church and told them that he was stopped for speeding. The officer only gave him a warning, and he wanted to thank him in front of the whole church for not making him any later. My sergeant then asked, "Why did you not write him a ticket?" I said, "Officer discretion." It is end of story.

For the most part, we drove Plymouth 440s as our patrol vehicle. They had dual exhaust and could go from zero to sixty in about two seconds (slight exaggeration). When you punched the gas, as the speed went up and the four barrels kicked in, you could almost watch the gas gauge go down.

One Christmas morning, I got into my vehicle and had to go to the city pumps to fill up. Just as I was nearing the gated area, I saw a vehicle driving out in an erratic manner. I figured he had been drinking. I pulled the vehicle over and approached, and the smell of the alcohol intoxicant reeked out of the vehicle. I had the gentleman get out, explained why I stopped him, and he said, "Please don't put me in jail on Christmas." He failed the sobriety test (walk the straight line, recite the alphabet, etc.) but continued to beg me not to put him in jail on Christmas. Using my "officer discretion," I called him a cab, told him to lock his vehicle, and come back at 4:00 p.m. to pick it up. I told him to go home and let it wear off. He said fine. I called a cab, watched him get in, and then followed the cab for a few blocks. I then remembered how I needed to get gas, but I was stopped by a person who was lost and needed directions to get downtown, so I told him how to get there.

When I got back to where the pumps were, I saw my previous drunk driver who "didn't want to be put in jail on Christmas" getting into his vehicle. I took off after him; we were doing a good 15 mph during the pursuit (lights and sirens). I called for a backup, and just as I got off the radio, we pulled into his driveway. He got out of his vehicle and said, "You can't do anything to me now; I am home," and he showed me his middle finger. Well, I then advised him that he was under arrest, at which he took a swing at me and we began fighting. We were rolling around in slush and snow, and it took a minute to gain control, but I did. As I was helping him up, Sergeant Roger showed up as my backup. He then called the guy by his first name (Roger had lived in the city for about thirty-five years and knew everybody); he asked him why he assaulted an officer. There was no answer. Roger looked at me (I had been on duty for an hour and my uniform looked like crap) and said, "After he goes to jail, go change your uniform."

Well, it turned out that the guy was a bigwig for the city. He was the midnight supervisor for snow removal, which was a *very* important job; if he had just been driving drunk, he may have only gotten his license suspended but could've used it for work purposes only, but the assaulting of a police officer cost him his job. I really didn't want to put him in jail on Christmas, but it was his choice.

Another time, I was following this guy on a four-lane road; he was in the fast lane doing twenty in a forty. I pulled him over and did not smell anything coming from the car. I looked at his driver's license, and the number was 1600. Now, my license number was 346,000. I asked him why he was going so slow, to which he replied that he just wasn't thinking. He then asked me if I was from the Midwest. I said yes. I asked him where he was from, and he said he left Cicero, Illinois, right after the Saint Valentine's Day Massacre. I told him where I was from, and he said that it was a "strip" capitol of Illinois. We laughed a bit, and I told him to drive carefully but move to the slow lane.

These traffic stops started out as routine, but let me tell you, they are never just routine. When you get out of the patrol vehicle, you are watching to see how many people are in the car, if they are doing anything suspicious, and what they are doing in the vehicle. Sergeant Roger always said, "No routine traffic stop is ever routine."

I came to work one morning and heard that Harry had been in an accident while on the midnight shift. Harry was with a reserve officer when they had stopped a guy for driving drunk, but while they were giving him the sobriety test in between the squad and the suspect's car, another drunk driver rear-ended the squad car. The reserve ended up with two broken legs, and the suspect had one broken leg. Harry was okay. From then on, we did the test alongside the road, not between the vehicles. The policy also changed that when you had to pull someone over at night in the winter, you need to turn your emergency lights off because the lights apparently attract drunks.

Because of the city I was in was considered "far from civilization," or just far from the lower forty-eight, the police would get a lot of long distance calls to go check on the caller's mother or father after they stated that they hadn't heard from them in a while. These calls were called "well-being, or welfare, checks." I was just finishing up having lunch at the "greasy spoon" restaurant with a couple of officers when I got a well-being check call. It was only about three blocks from where I was.

The apartments were a single-floor retirement community with about twenty-five apartments in the location. I went to the address and knocked on the door, and no one answered. I attempted to look through the living room window; the blinds were open just a bit. I could see someone in the recliner watching television. I went back and banged on the door harder, but the man did not move. I called for a supervisor, and Roger showed up a couple of minutes later. He looked in the window, mumbled some words, and told me to kick the door in. I hollered "police" and kicked the door in, which did not take much effort, and the smell inside was not good. Apparently, this guy had died a day or so ago watching TV. We called for the ambulance, and after it left, I went from door to door to try to get some answers. The neighbor next door said they had gone to the greasy spoon down the block the day before. He did not talk to him again after that. When the word got back to the police station where his last meal was (the police visited that place often), they quit going there for a long while. Cops, you see, are superstitious.

Remember the "trained observer" class that I talked about previously in "The Academy" chapter? I responded to an armed robbery at a bank where the suspect had left the scene. While I was waiting for the manager to rewind the videotape so I could watch it, I was talking to the tellers: "What did he look like?" "What race was he?" "Did he have a gun?" "Did he have a beard?" "How tall was he?" "How much did he weigh?" etc.? And all I kept getting was the same answer: "He was soooo big." I asked them what that meant, and they couldn't give me any details. Apparently, he had walked into the bank naked with no gun and no beard and just asked for the money. The tellers couldn't even tell me what race he was. They only saw one thing: his very large penis. They gave him the money, and he left.

Another time at the same bank, another officer and I were having lunch right next door. We got a call of an "armed robbery in progress." We advised them that we were right next door and to give us a suspect description. The description was young white male with a full beard. We left the restaurant; the officer I was with got her shotgun out of the patrol vehicle, and we walked across the parking lot. I unholstered my sidearm and had it ready at my side.

As we approached the front of the bank, which was about a five-second walk, a white male exited the bank, looked at us, and then jaywalked across the street nearly getting hit by a car. He looked suspicious, but no beard. I called dispatch and asked again for a description, and they said full beard. So not wanting to stop him, and possibly getting shot in the back, we blew him off and cautiously entered the bank after looking in the window.

"He just left!" they screamed. The other officer and I looked at each other and wondered how he had gotten away with us only a few seconds away. We waited for a supervisor and the FBI and then watched the tape. The FBI said no leads, so it was our case.

You see, the FBI at the time usually took the case over if there were leads, a suspect, and so on. But they did not believe there were any good leads. They only took on good cases, so their arrest and conviction percentages go up. If they don't take the case, then it doesn't go against their statistics.

Sergeant Roger showed up while I was interviewing the tellers, and we were getting ready to watch the video. And lo and behold, the guy on the video was the guy that we saw leaving the bank. A white guy with no beard was the suspect. I told Roger what I saw, and he said he also heard that the guy had a beard, but what could we do? We finished the witness statements and left the bank. About an hour later, I got a call of a defraud at a restaurant. The restaurant was the Mexican restaurant that the other officer and I had lunch at before the bank robbery. A defraud is when someone does not pay their bill and they just run away. I was talking to the manager, and she told me that this guy ate lunch and did not have money to pay his bill, so he left his driver's license as collateral and said he would be right back. Well, the picture on the license ended up being the same guy that robbed the bank!

I called the officer whom I had lunch with, along with Roger. He along with three more squads went to the guy's house, which was only two blocks away. My lunch partner and I walked up the front stairs with shotguns in hand while the other cars watched the side and back door. We knocked on the door, it opened, and the suspect put his hands up and surrendered without a struggle. What an easy felony arrest (that the FBI did not get). While interrogating the suspect, it turned out he went to lunch, had no money, was going to rob the bank and then come back and pay the bill. What upset his plan was the two of us coming from the same restaurant he had just eaten at so he had to leave the area.

Foot patrol was a lot of fun also. It was more PR than enforcing the law. Tourists would ask for directions while you were directing the "ladies" to another corner. The area that entailed foot patrol was about four blocks north and south by about six blocks east and west. It was strictly downtown, which took in the "dive bars," tourist sites, and downtown businesses.

One day, I was walking foot patrol, and I saw "Candy" (a regular streetwalker, hooker, etc.) talking to a foreign guy who just got off his ship. We had a lot of freighters drop off cargo at the port. I walked up to Candy and asked her what she was doing. She told me hello and that she was asking the man what time the bus was coming. I looked at the guy and asked him if it was true. By his accent, I could tell that he was Polish and did not speak much English. I told Candy that she had been working this corner long enough to know that buses didn't run down this street and that she should move along or could have a complimentary one-way trip to the station.

Later in the day, one of the street people, a female, came up to me and said that she had been raped. She was very intoxicated when she was talking to me. I clarified with her that she said raped, and she said yes and that she knew exactly who did it. I asked her who raped her, and she said it was "Red." Red was another street person. So we walked together for a while and found Red sleeping by a dumpster in the alley. I woke him up, and he looked a little startled. I asked him if he had raped this woman. He got up, and we walked a few feet away so he could give his side of the story. Red said that they were sharing some beers, and she got a little horny. She then wanted to get it on. He said okay. When they were done doing their thing by the dumpster, she said that would be fifty dollars. He said that the lay was not worth the fifty dollars. She told him that she was going to get him arrested for rape. I went back and asked her if Red's story was correct. She confirmed it. I told her that I would arrest Red but that she would also be under arrest for prostitution. She changed her mind and did not want to press charges. They left together, walking down the alley and holding each other up from falling. There was no paperwork on this case.

A lot of days when the shift was over, I had to unwind and talk about the day to someone. I couldn't talk to my wife because she didn't care. So when our shift would end, someone would usually suggest going out for a beer. I usually joined them.

We would go to a local pub and have a few and then have a few more. A lot of the guys were on their second or third wife, and they would say the same thing: "I can't talk to her. She won't listen." So we would listen to each other. We would laugh about the day's adventures and then listen to someone say that they almost screwed up that day. We would listen and then critique each other so if someone got into the same mess, he would know how to get out of it next time.

I think that if these guys were married to someone who listened, maybe they wouldn't be here right now. Then again, I am not a shrink, so what do I know? I do know one thing, that my wife did not care and she would not listen. Remember, she only wanted me to take the job that paid the most.

It is important for an officer to vent. Vent to your wife, vent to a neighbor, vent to your dog, or vent to another officer. What an officer sees in one week, most people would not see in their lifetime. Venting keeps a cop sane. Would you want to be stopped by a police officer that was not sane? You have to be a special breed to be a cop. You have to see something and then, as quickly as possible, blow it off because you're already on your way to another case. Yep, you have to be a special breed all right.

You will hear more about after-hours visits to the pubs in a later chapter.

Chapter 7

Traffic Stops

The traffic stops that I used as examples in the previous chapter were more like "You've got to hear about this one" incidents. In general, a traffic stop can be and sometimes is very dangerous.

Usually, in a city that has one-man officer cruisers, when the officer making the stop wants a backup unit, he calls for one. We had four codes for sending or requesting a unit. Below are the examples, then we will discuss the traffic stop.

Code 1: No lights or sirens. Very low priority. Take care of it when you are doing whatever you are doing. If something comes up with a higher priority while you are responding, take care of that first. A good example of a code 1 is a barking dog.

Code 2: You are to respond now; no lights or siren, but go now. The majority of calls are code 2 responses. Examples of code 2 responses are larceny, where the suspect was gone; burglary, where the suspect was gone; assault, where the victim was at the hospital, and so on.

Code 3: Lights and siren. Go now. Drop what you are doing. Life is in danger. But you are to proceed with caution. Examples of code 3 are someone with a weapon, an officer who is down, traffic accidents with injuries, etc.

Code 4: It is just as important as code 3 but no siren. Examples of code 4 are bank robbery in progress or a disturbance where life is in danger. The reason you are not using a siren is because you do not want the suspect to know you are on your way.

There is nothing wrong with calling for a backup unit on a traffic stop. A lot of police officers have been killed while making a traffic stop. You get a feeling, a "gut feeling," when you call for a backup unit. And when the unit is called for, you will usually tell them what code you want them to respond with.

I stopped a guy one time for speeding. There were two other people in the vehicle with my male driver. I called for a backup unit, code 2, and called in the license plate to dispatch. My backup was only a minute away, so I exited the cruiser and approached the driver. I asked for the necessary ID and registration. The driver was *really* nervous. I mean, a lot of drivers are nervous when stopped, but he was really bad. I told him that he was speeding, and he told me he would like to have a warning. I said why. He said, "Just because." He then told me that he would give me all the money he had (all he had was $13.87), and I could have it all if I let him go. I said nothing and went to my vehicle to run a check on him. Just then, my backup unit showed up. I told the officer to watch the vehicle while I ran a warrant check. Boy was I not surprised, it came back warrant. The driver was a marine deserter. The other officer and I approached the vehicle and told the driver to get out, and he was arrested. The two other passengers were told to exit the vehicle also.

When dispatch said there was a warrant for desertion, a couple more units showed up to help us out. While the other units were talking to the passengers, I searched, handcuffed, and placed the driver in the rear of the cruiser. I went back to the driver's vehicle, did a close hand search (that's anywhere that the driver could reach), and found a loaded .45-caliber pistol under the driver's seat. After the driver was processed at the jail, the MPs were called from my old unit, and they picked him up. The driver was charged with desertion, carrying a concealed weapon, and, oh yeah, I gave him a speeding ticket.

The traffic stop could have gone sour really quickly, but luckily, I think the show of force of the other units helped it come to a quiet close.

I was on routine patrol one afternoon driving through a residential neighborhood. I observed what I saw to be a possible drunken driver in front of me. He was not speeding, but he was driving across the whole road. I turned on my lights for him to stop, but he kept going. All of a sudden, he sideswiped two parked cars and then came to a stop. I called for a backup unit, code 3, because I was not sure if he was hurt. As I was getting out of my vehicle, a crowd of about ten to twenty African Americans started to stand around, screaming about the "honky" driver that just hit their cars. I called for more backup units with the chance that a riot may ensue. The driver was white, and the area he had the accident in was not. Four units were there in a minute or so, and I was tending to the driver who was passed out and slumped over the wheel. He seemed like he was drunk, but there were no signs of it in the vehicle. I could not smell any alcoholic intoxicants in the vehicle, but I did on his breath.

The paramedics showed up and attempted to talk to him. While this was going on, the crowd was getting rowdy and very verbal. The other units took care of the crowd so I could handle the driver and investigation. I was watching the paramedics give the driver a chocolate candy bar, and I was baffled. It turned out that the driver was not drunk but had a seizure from insulin. The candy bar brought him back around, and the crowd dispersed with a quiet end to a story that could've easily gotten out of hand.

I think the easiest traffic stop is to make a "felony stop." An officer knows from the beginning that it is going to be dangerous. When you are making a "routine stop," you do not know what you are getting yourself into. A felony stop, you know, this is the "big one"; you are expecting the worst.

We got a call from a wife that after an argument, her husband left the house with a bunch of guns, and she did not know what he was going to do. She gave dispatch the vehicle information and a detailed description of her husband. While on patrol, I saw the vehicle. I followed it and notified dispatch for backup, code 4, and that I would be stopping the vehicle in an area where businesses were closed for the day. I saw my backup coming up behind me, along with two patrol cars in front of me at an intersection, so I knew I could pull him over. When my backup got close, I turned on my lights. The vehicle pulled over, my backup pulled alongside of me, and the two patrols in front came at us.

We all exited our vehicles, with shotguns at the ready, standing behind our opened driver door. I told the driver to exit the vehicle and lay facedown on the street with his arms out. There was a brief lapse, and then I repeated the order. The driver came out of his vehicle, hands up, and laid in the street just like asked. While the officers watched him, I went forward, searched, and cuffed him. Then he was helped up off the street and asked what the problem was. He said that he and his wife got into an argument, and he took his guns out of the house for safety. We searched the vehicle, and he had a few guns in the trunk, along with some dynamite and a .410 rifle that had the barrel sawed down so it was no bigger than a pistol. He was arrested for the .410 and the dynamite. An ATF (alcohol, tobacco, and firearms) agent came to the station and took control of the .410 and the dynamite. Luckily, this one turned out with a happy ending.

You drive down the street, and you see a police car pulled over, lights on, and another vehicle in front. *Oh, he pulled someone over,* you think. Well, it is not as easy as you think. Before I exit the vehicle, I have called in the plates, checked how many people are in the vehicle, see if they are doing anything suspicious with their hands, called for a backup unit, and then exited my vehicle.

While walking to the vehicle, I make sure I am not in his side mirror, watching everyone in the vehicle. If it is a van, I will walk to the corner of the vehicle, in the front, so I can look at everybody in the vehicle. You know when you see a van with those cool, tinted windows? Those windows are a nightmare for a police officer. You cannot see in the vehicle; you do not know how many people are in the vehicle; it is a nightmare waiting to happen.

As Sergeant Roger always said, "A routine stop is never routine."

Chapter 8

The Unknown Disturbance

There is a list of statistics that are kept about police officer deaths, and at the top of that list is disturbance calls.[2] Why are so many police officers killed on disturbance calls? I would guess that they don't think about getting killed there. They let their guard down. Could it be apathy? "Oh, it's only a husband and wife fighting it out."

When I went through the academy, we were told that the number one way for an officer to be killed in the line of duty was "the unknown disturbance." Now, here we are sometime later, and the justice department statistics states that between 1976 and 1998, (when this book was originally started), the number one way for a police officer to get killed was at 16%. To update those stats, between 2010 and 2014, the percentage of policer officers being killed at a domestic rose to 22 percent.[3] Why is this number so high? Do police officers drop their guard?

You would think that if an officer does not know what is going on, he would have his guard *up*, but apparently not.

Like I was talking about in the previous chapter, I think the felony traffic stop is the easiest stop to make. You know you have felons,

---

2   US Department of Justice, Bureau of Justice Statistics.
3   US Department of Justice, Bureau of Justice Statistics.

and they may be armed. But at a disturbance call, a husband and wife fighting, why are cops getting killed so often?

I was responding to an unknown disturbance call with a backup unit. The wife called for police. There were no guns in the house that the wife told dispatch. We arrived and cautiously walked up the stairs to the front door. Now, you *never* stand in front of the door when you knock. We stood off to the side of the door, and I tapped on the screen.

A woman in her thirties came to the door, bleeding from the mouth, and I could see that she was missing a couple of teeth. She screamed, "Throw the bastard in jail!" We observed a male, the husband, sitting on the living room couch. We asked the woman if she wanted us to call the paramedics. All she kept saying was to throw the bastard in jail.

I started to talk to the husband, and the other officer took the woman into the kitchen so he could talk to her. The husband told me that he had got home from work late because he had stopped off at a bar with some coworkers. I asked him if he called his wife to let her know that he would be late. He said he did not, and when he got home two hours past his normal time, he walked in the front door and his wife slapped him across the face. I asked him what did he do then, and he said he busted her in the chops. Right after he said that, his wife screamed again to throw him in jail.

Well, not to be undone, he started screaming back at her, at which time he stood up, and I told him to sit back down. He sat on the couch and started screaming at his wife over my shoulder. She, in turn, started screaming back. He stood up again, and I told him to sit down. This getting up and down went on a few more times when all of a sudden, he attempted to push me out of the way. He started screaming at his wife saying he was going to knock the crap out of her. He and I started to struggle, and the other officer came into the room to help me get the cuffs on him for assaulting a police officer. While we had him on his stomach on the couch, the wife came out of the kitchen screaming, "Leave my husband alone!" and stabbed the other officer in the shoulder with a butcher knife. Luckily, his bulletproof vest stopped the knife, and he turned with his knife still in his shoulder and hit the wife in the mouth, causing her to lose two more teeth. He then put her in cuffs.

What started out as a husband and wife disturbance turned into assaulting a police officer and assault with a deadly weapon. Now, did we do wrong? He should have stayed with her while I was fighting with the husband? A police officer has to make a split-second decision to react to something, and hopefully, it is the right decision. We were once told in the academy that it is better to be judged by twelve (by a jury if it is the wrong decision) than to be carried by six (pallbearers). A police officer makes a split decision and has to live with it. Months down the road, his defense attorney can be a Monday night quarterback and try to prove that it was the wrong decision.

Most of the time, the officer gets it right, but to have an attorney in court three or six months later, telling a jury that he should have or should not done this because of x, y, z, is an uneasy situation if they have not been in the officer's shoes.

The reason for an "unknown disturbance" can range from "She burned the turkey" to "He/she is cheating on me." Do not put your guard down for any reason. More police are shot or killed at an unknown disturbance than any other way.

I came to work one morning and was told there was a husband and wife disturbance on the swing shift (4:00 p.m.–2:00 a.m.). When the officers arrived and were walking up to the house, the husband shot at them with a rifle. They called for backup, and to quote an office, "All hell broke loose." When another squad car showed up, the husband put a couple of rounds through the vehicle.

The officers closed off the street and were attempting to get the people who lived across, and next to him, out of their houses for their own safety. The guy shot up four police cars. Once the area was secure, and no bystanders were in danger, the command was made to wait him out.

Well, before you knew it, the midnight shift (10:00 p.m.–8:00 a.m.) came on. The officers had to exchange places with the old shift so they could get off. While this was happening, every once in a while, he would pop off another round, just to let everyone know that he was still there. The decision was made to continue to wait him out and that sooner or later, he was going to get sleepy and doze off. Then the officers could storm his place and take him into custody.

Well, now it was day shift's turn (8:00 a.m.–6:00 p.m.) to take over the scene. I was on perimeter duty about two houses away making sure the road was not crossed by pedestrians. It had been almost sixteen hours since this thing had gone down, and there he was in the window, popping off a round every once in a while. Then things turned for the worst, and an officer was wounded in the leg. The suspect came to the window with his wife and said he was going to kill her if we did not leave. He was holding a pistol to her head.

The decision was made. We needed to end this before anyone else got hurt. A police officer sharpshooter was brought in and put into position. He was told that if there were more shots fired and if the wife was not in danger, to take him out. Well, the suspect came to the window and started screaming at the officers and firing his pistol at them. There was one shot from the police officer, and it was over.

Now, let's go back to the beginning when the officers arrived. Shots were fired at them, and they took cover. They were responding to an unknown disturbance. Were they in defensive mind when they were walking up to the house? Were they thinking, oh gee, another husband and wife thing? Is this why more police officers are killed at a disturbance than any other way?

Not all disturbance calls turn out bad. Some are just about two people arguing, it gets out of hand, and someone calls the police. But officers do not know about this before they get there. Should they not treat them like a traffic stop involving a van with tinted windows? He does not know who is involved or how many people are involved. This way, he does not drop his guard.

I was responding to an unknown disturbance. My backup unit was Sergeant Roger. I got there first, and Sergeant Roger showed up a few seconds later. As we started to walk toward the front door, he told me to unsnap my holster. I said that I always do. He said to be prepared for this one. He knew the husband and wife. The husband was an owner of a Tae Kwon Do martial arts business. He was a tenth-degree black belt. He said that he would handle the talking, but be prepared. He said forty hours of defensive training in police academy was not enough for this guy. He could probably kill us both and not even work up a sweat.

We then walked up to the front door and knocked. A male voice said to come in. When you hear that, you never, never walk in. Wait for someone to open the door. A very large Asian male came to the door, and Roger, calling him by his first name, asked him how he was doing. Roger, I think, knew everybody in Anchorage. I think Roger moved there in about 1800, not really but it sure seemed that way. He said fine. He then asked him how his wife was doing, and he said not well. She had burned dinner, there was an argument, and he slapped her. Roger asked where she was, and he replied, "In the bathroom." Roger called to her and asked her to come out, which she did. She had a very swollen black-and-blue right eye. She said that she wanted to press assault charges against her husband. Roger told him to turn around and put his hands behind his back so he could cuff him. The husband said that he didn't want to. Roger told him that if he didn't, then we would have to fight, and the husband would end up killing us both; and in order to keep that from happening, either he should put his hands behind his back or the other officer (me) would shoot him. He put his hands behind his back, and I cuffed him. This was a great example of "the bluff." The suspect did not know if Roger was bluffing or not.

Roger was right, though. All the defensive training in the world would not have been enough for this guy. Would I have shot him if he didn't comply? We will never know, but I am glad that Roger was there and knew him.

Not all victims are the wife, you know. I responded with a backup unit to a disturbance that the "husband" called into the police. The husband was in the Army and lived in town with his wife. He was on a three-day "in the field training exercise" and came home to his drunk wife. The husband came home early because he had broken his right leg. Now, this couple was going at it when we got there. They were outside by the porch, and the drunken wife was kicking her husband's leg casts, and she was barefoot. He was a little guy at about five feet and 140 pounds. She was five feet, six inches and about 350 pounds. We pulled up, and she had him pinned against the railing and was kicking the poop out of his cast.

When we arrived, she stopped kicking him, looking at us walking up the sidewalk, and then went back to kicking him some more. When I got close to her, and I could see that there were no weapons, I told her that that was enough. She turned toward me and took a swing at me with a closed right fist. I backed up, and due to her high concentration of an alcoholic intoxicant, she missed and landed face first on the sidewalk. We rolled her over and helped her sit up. She started cussing at us and never stopped. The husband said he did not want to press charges. I told him he did not need to since both of us officers saw her kicking him. She then said that after we left, she was going to kill him in his sleep. The husband said he would press charges.

We had to use three pairs of handcuffs because she could not bring her arms far enough back. Both of us officers always carried extra, so that was not a problem. The only funny thing about the whole thing was that we never found out why she got drunk. She would not tell us.

Not all unknown disturbances turn out bad. Usually, they involved three things: him, her, and alcohol. Roger and I responded to a disturbance, and when we got there, both people were crying. Roger was there first, so he handled the call. Upon talking to both intoxicated people, it was determined that they were not happy with each other. They had been friends for five years and then lived together for three years. The decision was made that they would get married.

According to both parties, that was the biggest mistake they had made. So Roger, with his "we can fix this situation" personality, asked them if they would be happier if they were not married. They both agreed. So Roger called both of them up to him. "Place your right hand on my badge," he stated. They both complied. "By the power vested to me as a police officer, I hereby divorce you both immediately." They looked at each other, kissed each other, and said thank you. Roger and I left, and *never* we got another call from that address again. You really *cannot* make this stuff up.

There are four examples of unknown disturbances: one turned out bad for the suspect, and officers could have been hurt or killed; one had two people go to jail, and an officer could have been killed; in the third case, no officers were hurt or injured; and finally, the fourth, everyone left happy.

You cannot take a chance when you go to a disturbance. You have to have your head on straight and in the game. The life you save may be yours or someone else's.

Chapter 9

Kids

I think talking about children with police work is a tough subject. Why? Because you are a married cop with kids and you get involved in a kid case. It really hits home.

I had a few cases involving kids, and none of the cases turned out good. They were devastating to me, and when I got home to talk to my wife, all I got was, "Don't bring your work home." I am really surprised that with the pressures at work and then to go home to not much of anything at home, I remained faithful to her and never cheated. And I mean that; I really didn't.

I was on routine patrol and sent to a traffic accident with injuries that was a code 3. When I arrived at the scene, I noticed a two-vehicle, head-on collision. I approached the scene after calling for a backup unit for traffic control. The driver of vehicle two, a female, told me that her three-year-old daughter was in the front seat, and she could not get the seat belt off.

As I approached the vehicle, it started to catch on fire. The mother started screaming to get her daughter out. I forced the passenger door open, but the seat belt was jammed. I called to the daughter, but she did not answer. I reached for my Buck knife on my belt and cut the seat belt. It was at this time that I noticed that the little girl was dead. I picked her up and took her away from the burning car.

This is when I discovered that it felt like every bone in her body was broke. Her body was like a rag doll. The fire department showed up to put the fire out. While I was placing the girl on the gurney, the driver of the other vehicle came up to me, screaming: "I'm bleeding to death; get the paramedics!" I looked over at him, and all I could see was a cut over his left eye. I didn't really feel bad for this guy, with what looked like a minor injury, wanted me to drop everything so I could take care of *him*.

The mother went to the hospital with the daughter. The daughter did not make it. She was declared DOA (dead on arrival) even though I knew she was dead on the scene. I approached the male driver of the other vehicle and detected a strong odor of an alcoholic intoxicant emanating from his breath. A second paramedic van showed up to give him first aid, but he refused transportation to the hospital. I was sort of glad because after he failed the sobriety test, I gave him a free ride to jail. He was booked into jail and charged with vehicular homicide.

I was glad that I was at the end of my shift because this case had really hit me hard. I talked to a couple of the guys when I was leaving work, and they wanted me to go out for a few. I told them no and that all I wanted to do was go home and hug my three-year-old daughter. It was about 8:00 p.m. when I got home, and my wife was watching television. I told her that I had a really bad day, and she replied that she did not want to hear about it. I walked into my daughter's bedroom and looked at her sleeping so soundly. I walked up to her bed, picked her up, and gave her a big hug. She woke up for a second and said, "Daddy." As I was laying her back on the bed, my wife came into the bedroom screaming at me: "What the fuck are you doing? You are going to wake her!" I just looked at her, then again at my daughter, and then back at my wife and said, "You will never understand."

I think besides getting a radio dispatch to an unknown disturbance, the second scariest call is "Baby not breathing" or "Baby blue." This call makes me shiver. I know when I get to the house, there is going to be mad hysteria. And the problem I will have is, after the paramedics leave, I am treating the hysterical parent or parents as suspects until the autopsy comes back as a SIDS (sudden infant death syndrome) or an unknown cause. There is always that possibility that the baby was shaken to death, smothered, or who knows what happened.

I responded to two that I can recall, and it is not a good feeling. My first one was the toughest. I still remember it like it was yesterday. The mother told me that her three-month-old baby was sick, and she laid it down to sleep. When the mom woke up in the morning, she went to check on the infant, and it was blue. She started to give it mouth-to-mouth, but it did not wake up, so she called the police.

The father was out of town, so I only interviewed the mother. I noticed that the baby had no signs of trauma when the paramedics took it away. The mother said it was her first child, and she did not know what happened. She said the baby had been sick the night before, gave the baby some medicine, and laid it down. She asked me what was going to happen next, and I told her that because the baby died under mysterious circumstances, they would have to perform an autopsy. She said she called her husband, and he would catch a flight and be back in town in two days. I told her thank you and asked her if there was anyone that I could call to stay with her. She said her neighbor was going to come over in a few minutes.

The next day was my day off, but I had to go to the autopsy of the baby. When I got to the morgue, the medical examiner was ready to start. I had my camera in case I had to take pictures if there were signs of trauma or any unknown marks on the baby.

This autopsy was performed just like the one I saw in the academy. But seeing that little thing laying there on that big stainless table was incredibly hard on me. I watched the ME looking over the body, and he couldn't find any signs of trauma. He then began the autopsy; took a piece of the liver, the heart, and the lung; and put them into a dish. He did a few other things, and after what seemed like forever, he said he was done. I asked him for the cause of death. He said pending the tox report (that was from the samples he took), it looked to him like SIDS (Sudden Infant Death Syndrome). I felt relieved, but I also felt the major loss for the parents.

I went home after the autopsy, and all my wife could say was, "Why do you bother to come home? You should just sleep there." I did not go any further or make any comments about the baby.

Another day, I responded to a suicide. I arrived at the residence and was met by a woman that lived there. She said that she and her boyfriend's son were home, and the boyfriend was out of state on business. She came home and called for the son, and he did not answer. She went into his bedroom and found him dead. A next-door neighbor came over to console her, so I excused myself and went into the boy's bedroom.

When I entered the room, I saw the boy sitting on his bed, his feet on the floor, and a rifle between his legs with the barrel in his mouth. I also noticed that the boy was barefoot. The paramedics arrived and examined the body, and another officer came and took pictures of how the boy was positioned.

Upon examining the rifle, it was a .22-caliber long rifle. Only one bullet had been discharged. The boy apparently had stuck the rifle in his mouth and then pulled the trigger with his big toe. Because the bullet was a small caliber, there was not enough force to knock his body over; it just slumped onto the barrel of the rifle. There were brains all over the bed.

After the body was taken away, I went back and talked to the woman. She told me that a couple of weeks ago, the boy had been picked up for shoplifting along with a few of his friends. When his father found out, he forbade him from seeing any of those kids anymore. He told his son that they were a bad influence on him. That morning, the boy had cut school and was caught shoplifting again. The girlfriend went to pick him up and told him that he would be in trouble because he was still hanging out with the kids that his dad told him to stay away from. When she brought him home, she told him to go to his room and think about what he was going to tell his dad.

She said she went to go take a shower, and when she came down to talk to him, she found him dead. She then called the police. She said that twice he was picked up for shoplifting, and both times, she was watching him while his dad was out of town. She said when his dad came home, he was probably going to kick her out. I gave her some phone numbers of family crisis groups and told her that if his dad or she had any questions to give me a call. I finished my paper-work, waited for the paramedics, and then left the residence.

I responded to another suicide with a different story. A young boy came home early from school and let himself into the house. His father was out of town, and his live-in girlfriend was home. The boy went into his bedroom, put a rifle into his mouth, like the previous boy, and killed himself. End of story? Wrong. Upon me talking to the girlfriend, she was not very cooperative in the beginning. I found out that the boy heard a noise in his dad's/girlfriend's bedroom. He opened the door to investigate and saw the girlfriend in bed doing her thing with a different guy than his father. She saw him at the door. The boy who really liked the girlfriend probably figured that if his dad found out, she would get thrown out of the house. So instead, he went to his bedroom and blew his brains out.

The girl finally told me the story, and all she cared about was that I did not put in the report that she was screwing around with someone else. I told her that I would write the report as I saw it.

When a police officer goes to a call of a juvenile suicide, he thinks to himself, *What caused it to be so bad that he had to take his own life?* Then he has to forget about it. If a police officer was to keep everything that he saw bottled up inside, he would explode. I believe that is why you need to keep a sense of humor. I think that is what kept me from going bonkers. I would see all this stuff, come home, and not be able to tell my wife anything because she did not care. So I started to laugh it off. Don't get me wrong; I wouldn't laugh where people could see me. It was more to myself, a valve, so to speak. This brings me to another story about kids that had everybody laughing but me.

I was responding to a shelter run by the Salvation Army for an assault. The shelter was for runaways and pregnant teens that had been kicked out of their house or just couldn't live with their parents anymore.

I walked into the reception area and was met by a counselor who had been assaulted by one of the runaways. She turned and pointed to a female that was about sixteen quietly sitting on a bench in the waiting area. I took the counselor's statement and advised her that the girl would be going to juvenile detention for three days. The counselor said fine with her.

I walked up to the girl, introduced myself, and told her to stand up, turn around, and put her hands behind her back. The girl leaped off the bench and had both her hands around my neck in a second. We went to rolling around on the floor and up against the reception desk. I saw out of the corner of my eye the desk phone go flying off the desk as we bumped into it. Finally, I was able to grab her, pick her up, and body-slam her to the floor. I rolled her onto her stomach, put the cuffs on. Finally, the police academy hand-to-hand training I received had helped. I told the counselor to add the police assault that she witnessed. The counselor said fine, then reached for a paper towel, and was going to wipe the side of my face. I took the paper towel, held it to the right side of my face, pulled it away, and saw a blood line about six inches long. I asked the counselor if she had a mirror, and she took one out of her desk. I looked at the right side of my face, and I had a scratch that started below my right ear and went to the center of my chin.

I called my sergeant (Roger), and he told me to go to the hospital after she was put in detention. I dropped her off, went to the hospital, got a shot for infection and a tetanus shot, and was told to watch out the next time. I thought to myself how funny it was that I just got my butt kicked by a juvenile. It was now the end of my shift, and I was in the squad room doing my paperwork. Roger walked in, and he began to tell everyone that I got my butt whipped by a little kid. The peer pressure was unbelievable.

I had to put up with it for three days, but I got the last laugh. While on patrol, I heard a unit being sent to the shelter on an assault. When I called dispatch, they confirmed it was the same girl, and I told them to send a backup unit. Some of the units listening on the radio made sly comments, but a backup unit was sent. That same girl went ballistic, and it took both officers to get her in cuffs. She went back into detention for three days.

At the end of the shift, the two officers were talking like they had fought a brown bear. They were discussing how tough and wiry she was. I just listened and kept my mouth shut.

Three days later, another assault call came from the center; and yes, it is the same girl. This time, two units were sent, and Sergeant Roger went to see who the girl was. He said he wanted to see who the girl was that was beating up his officers. Well, she went ballistic again, and it took all three of them to get her in cuffs. No one ever said anything to me again. Remember, I had her in cuffs all on my own. There were no more jokes about me getting my butt kicked by a juvenile ever again.

It is important to keep your guard up at all times. You never know who is going to have an attitude with an officer. I called my father after the first incident and told him that it was *his* fault that I got whipped by this little female. He asked why, and I told him that he was the one that told me to respect women; and because of that, she got in the first punch. He laughed, and then we laughed together. There are no male suspects and no female suspects. They are all suspects, *period.*

Chapter 10

Off-Duty Stuff

A police officer has a very tedious, emotional, and strenuous job. When you get a day off, take it. Do not volunteer to work overtime (unless you really, really need the money) or do things at the department. If you are off and married, spend time with your family. When I was on the force, due to our massive expansion, we had a lot of overtime. I took it whenever they called. There was a time that lasted about a year where I was working about five to six days a week even though I was hired to work four tens.

At that time, I believed that this was one factor that caused tension in the marriage. Later, in my case, I found out that it wasn't true. My wife just did not care at all about what I did or when I did it.

Even though we were police officers twenty-four hours a day, we had an unwritten policy on days off: Do not get involved in anything unless it was a felony. If you saw something, call the police. Sounds easy, doesn't it? Well, things do not always sound as good as they are. Below are a couple of examples where "Look the other way" doesn't always work.

When an officer moves into a neighborhood, people see this and they remember. They will come up and ask you anything from an accident they saw on the news to "Can you fix a ticket for your neighbor?" I tried to keep silent about stuff that happened on the news, and I never fixed a ticket. Be nice, listen, and then move on.

I was home one night in the twelve-apartment complex that we lived in. I heard a scream for someone to call the police. The first thing I did was grabbed my off-duty revolver and then went to the front door. I saw and heard a lady crying, so I went down to find out what was going on. She said her boyfriend tried to commit suicide, and she just called the paramedics.

I followed her to her apartment and saw her boyfriend sitting in a recliner, bleeding from the right arm. I immediately took off my belt and placed it around his right bicep. I made it very tight like a tourniquet. When I tightened the belt enough to stop the bleeding, I could see five or six slices across his arm. The gashes were very deep because on two of them, you could see the bone. I held the belt tight for about a minute and told the girl to get a couple of towels. She wrapped the arm in the towels while I held the belt. I was attempting to talk to him, but he was very drunk. I noticed six-packs of empty bottles next to the recliner.

After about three or four minutes, the paramedics showed up. They removed my belt and used one of their own straps. The girl went to the hospital in the ambulance. A few days later, I saw the guy and asked him what happened. He told me that he was fired from work because he was coming to work drunk. He said he did not know where they got their information from because he hardly drank. They moved out of the apartment complex about a week later, and I never saw them again.

I know this was not a felony, but someone had to save that person's life. She was too hysterical to do anything, and no one else was around. So that left me. Luckily, I didn't have to do any paperwork since it was strictly a medical call.

Because I love the cold, crisp air, my wife and I had an agreement. I could sleep with the window open (even in the winter), and she could have the waterbed (remember them?) as high as she wanted. So the window was opened about four inches, and the waterbed was set to ninety.

One winter night about 2:00 a.m., I heard the dog barking and jumping on the bed. I opened my eyes and could see my breath in my bedroom.

I glanced over toward the left and saw my wife looking out from our second-story window. We recently moved to a better part of town where there were a bunch of fourplexes. I asked her what she was doing, and she said that she heard a noise, went to the window, and saw these two guys breaking into parked cars, stealing stereos and CB radios.

I called 911, told them that I was a police officer, and told dispatch what was going on. Dispatch told me that due to a fresh snow-fall, there were a lot of accidents, and it would be awhile before an officer would show up. I told dispatch that I would respond but let the responding officers know that there would be an off-duty officer on the scene with a gun and to not get trigger-happy. Because Anchorage was expanding so rapidly, officers were constantly being hired, and we didn't always recognize all the officers on other shifts. She said she would. I got dressed, grabbed my revolver and both sets of handcuffs, and then put on my coat. Before I left, I grabbed my flashlight. It was dark out, and the closest streetlight was about four houses away.

I went outside and stopped by the corner of my building so I could get a good view of how many people were there. I observed two males, eighteen to twenty years old, prying open the car doors and taking out the stereos and CB radios and a third suspect in one of the vehicles that was getting broken into. When I was positive there was no one else, I drew my revolver, turned on the flashlight, and yelled out, "Police! Freeze!" The two men froze in their tracks. I approached them and asked them what they were doing. They did not answer. I looked over by one of the parked cars, and I observed about six stereos and a few CB radios in a pile on the snow. I asked them if anyone else was helping them, and they said no. I then had the third guy get out of the vehicle he was in. I was going to ask them for ID, but I hesitated a minute because I didn't want them to leave the scene. I had them get into a push-up position in the snow and then walked and handcuffed one guy's wrist to the other, and then, with the second set of cuffs I had with me, I handcuffed the second guy to the final suspect. I then patted them down for weapons, which they did not have, and found their wallets with IDs. While I was surveying their booty, one of the guys said to the other guy, "Why didn't you tell me a cop lived on this block?" The other one answered that he didn't know there was a cop living there.

Well, about ten minutes later, a police vehicle showed up; the officer, whom I did not know, asked me a few questions, then used his cuffs, and put them in the car after searching them again. I handed him their IDs, and he told me to come down to the station to make a report. I said fine. We took all the stereos/CBs and put them into the officer's trunk. I followed him to the station and did the end of my paperwork while he put them in detention.

It was now getting close to the time for day shift to come to work, but it was my day off. In walked Sergeant Russ, one of my sergeants. He asked me that wasn't I busy enough that I had to go out and find trouble? We laughed, and he said, "Let me get you a coffee." I left a short time later. When I got home, I told my wife that I got five hours overtime; and she replied, "So what?"

When an officer is "off duty," it is exactly that—off duty. You can almost say off duty is like being an undercover officer. You do not want people to know you are an officer. When you are in civilian clothes, you sometimes see things that a uniformed officer would not see. You do not want to brag that you are a cop.

We had an incident where a rookie officer and his wife went grocery shopping. When the wife was writing a check, she saw that she did not have her ID with her. After writing the check, she told her husband to use his ID. The husband pulled out his badge and showed it to the clerk.

The clerk said that it was nice, but she needed to see a driver's license. The officer responded, "This is all you need to see." The clerk called for a manager. The manager arrived and asked what the problem was. She explained that the gentleman would not produce a driver's license, just his badge. The manager explained it was store policy to have a driver's license with the check. The officer said this was his badge, and that was all the manager needed to see. The manager did not argue anymore with the officer. He took down his badge number and wrote it on the check. The officer and his wife left the store with their groceries.

The manager called the police department and talked to the chief of police. He told the chief of the problem he had with the officer. The chief said he would take care of it. The officer was called into the chief's office the next time he came to work and was suspended for three days without pay for being a jerk. He was never a really good cop. He later resigned from the force.

Speaking of groceries, one day while off, my wife and I were coming home with a trunk full of groceries. We were traveling east on a divided highway. I just got my car up to the speed limit after stopping for a red light when I saw a car coming from the left. It blew the stop sign from the west traffic and then blew the stop sign for the east traffic. I thought to myself, *There is going to be an accident.* I told my wife to hold on. Now came the decision I had to make; either I floored it and hoped she missed me, or I locked up my brakes and I hit her broadside. I made the decision to floor it and stomp on the gas. I saw her coming, and just then, she hit us on the driver's side behind the driver's door. The impact was so hard; I felt the car spin on two wheels and came to a rest facing westbound. The impact spun us around 180 degrees.

When the car came to a stop, I asked my wife if she was okay. She said she was sore. I had hit my head on the driver's door window. We got out of the car, and I walked up to the other driver and asked her if she was all right. She told me that she was okay but a little shaken up. I asked her what happened, and she said her foot had slipped off the brake. I thought to myself, *Yeah, twice.* Some people standing by their house called the police. My shift was on duty at the time. My wife got out of the car, ran up to this little old lady, and said, "You better have fucking insurance!"

A few minutes later, two patrol cars showed up. They asked what happened, and I told them. The lady got out of her car and walked up to my wife. She saw me talking to the officers and asked my wife if I was a police officer. My wife said, "Yes, he is a fucking cop!" The woman was given two tickets for the two stop signs she forgot to stop at. My car was totaled.

When you are on duty, be a cop. When you are off duty, be a John Doe citizen. There are enough police officers out to handle the caseload when you are off. That is why it is called a day off. Take your day off and be off and unwind. It will be less pressure on your relationship. When my wife was busy with other things, I would go to the gym and play racket ball with one of my buddies. Don't go looking for trouble; if trouble is meant for you, it will find you.

An off-duty police officer, wife, and two daughters were getting ready to walk into a bank when the doors flung open. Two men with masks and shotguns told the four of them to lie on the sidewalk. They complied. The two men ran to an old 1968 Chevy and burned rubber out of the parking lot. The officer withdrew his off-duty 9 mm and pelted the rear window with numerous holes. It never even slowed them down. I preferred the .357.

Chapter 11

The Silent Badge: Officer Down/Injured or Dead

One day, I was getting ready to go to work, and my wife said, "Don't be late. I'm going to a candle party when you get home." I told her she had enough candles, and all they did was collect dust. We argued back and forth awhile, and finally, I had to leave for work.

I was driving around, thinking to myself about why she needed candles. Sure, they looked nice, but they are not used for burning. They just sat around and collected dust, not counting how much those things cost; some were over forty dollars in price, and why, she had to have them. Well, I had looked at my watch, and it was almost time to head for the station. It had been a pretty quiet day.

I was following this pickup truck that had a bunch of fifty-five-gallon drums in the back. He swerved to get into the left turn lane, and one of the barrels fell down in the back of the pickup and then rolled down the street. All of a sudden, I saw this dark-blue smoke or steam coming out of the drum. I turned my lights on and called for a fire truck. I tried to catch the driver's license plate, but he turned and kept going.

I called it in to dispatch as a possible hazardous spill. Roger got on the radio and asked me if I needed help with traffic control. I told him that I did, but I didn't know what I was dealing with. The fire department arrived, and the captain took out his thick book of chemicals. He found the one that he was looking for. He said they were going to foam it down, then come back in thirty minutes, and hose it into the sewer. Roger pulled up, heard the conversation that I had with the fire captain, and told me to go downwind while he would go upwind to control traffic. Everything went okay. Thirty minutes later, the fire department came back and hosed the foam into the sewer, and Roger and I went back to the station.

As I was driving to the station, I felt like I was getting dizzy. I was having trouble controlling the vehicle. I called Roger and asked him if he was okay. He said he was fine and why. I told him how I felt, and he told me to pull over and that he would request a paramedic van to my location. I told him that I would be passing the firehouse that the captain came from, and I would stop in and see the paramedics.

I arrived at the firehouse, parked my car, and staggered into the station. I found the captain and asked him about the stuff that they had foamed down and sent into the sewers. He asked why I was inquiring. I told him that I was not feeling well and wanted to know what the stuff was. He got out his thick book, found the page, and recited to me what it said: "Dangerous, flammable, do not open in a closed room." He said that I did not look well, and he got one of the paramedics to look at me. The paramedic said that I needed to go to the hospital immediately, and I agreed. I said that I would drive there because it was only a block from the firehouse, but he told me no that they would take me. I was starting to feel worse, so I didn't argue. I called Roger and told him that I was leaving my vehicle at the firehouse and was being transported to the hospital, code 3. He said that he was on his way.

When we got to the emergency room, they were waiting for me. The first thing that they did was put me on 100 percent oxygen. They took me to a room and started to draw blood. I asked them what was going on. No one would tell me anything. Roger showed up, took control of my weapon, and then asked me for the keys to my patrol car. I told him that I wouldn't be there long, and he said we would see.

A doctor came in while I was talking to Roger and told me that if I would've waited ten more minutes, I would have been dead. I asked why, and he said that the blue stuff was dry cleaning fluid concentrate and because I had inhaled it, the stuff had taken almost all the oxygen out of my blood. The doctor told me that my oxygen level in my blood should be anywhere from 90 to 95 percent; mine was at 73 percent. He said I was going to have to stay on oxygen for at least three to four hours and have someone draw my blood once an hour. Only when my oxygen level returned to normal would I be released from care. He then told me that I had to take off my clothes so they could bag them up; I would have to have my wife come out with fresh clothes. Roger said he would have dispatch send a unit to my house. I told him that she was going to be really pissed at me; I told him about the candle party. He laughed and said, "Look how much money you saved!" I said, "Yeah, right."

About an hour later, in walked my wife with a scowl on her face. I asked her if she knew what happened and she said yes. She then looked at me and said, "You did this on purpose so I couldn't go to the candle party!" She never once asked me if I was okay. About four hours later, the blood test said that I was fine, so I got dressed, and she took me home. We did not say a word to each other the whole trip home. Yeah, I did it on purpose so she couldn't go to the candle party.

One morning, I came to work and I saw Harry doing some paperwork in the squad room. He was on midnight shift. I hadn't seen him in a while, and I asked him how he was doing. He told me to meet him for coffee later and that he wanted to talk to me. A few hours later, I stopped at a coffee shop and asked him what was going on. He told me that he was going to file for a divorce and not to say anything to my wife or his until she got the paperwork. I said sure, fine. He said that they weren't talking and that things weren't going well. We finished our coffee and were walking out the door when he told me it was a real bummer that she was going to get half of everything. It just didn't seem fair. I told him that they had been married a long time, way back to when we were MPs together. There wasn't much he could do about it. He said, "Yeah, I guess so."

About a week later, I was walking into the squad room, and there were a few guys from midnights talking to a couple of guys from my shift; I went up to them and asked them what was going on. The guys from midnights told me that Harry had been killed that morning. I asked them how it had happened. They said that he was responding to a gas station fire and went through an intersection, and due to icy road conditions, he lost control and hit a light pole. The vehicle exploded on contact. I was devastated. The rest of the shift came in, and they were given the news.

While going through the night's actions, Roger told anybody that did not hear the news. He said that the investigation was still pending, but it looked like speed and icy roads were the contributing factors. He gave us a lecture about how speed will kill you if you do not keep your head on straight. He also said that Harry's vehicle was in the city lot by the gas pumps, and he wanted the whole shift to go and look at it. "Speed kills," he said. We finished briefing; I got my vehicle and went down to get gas and see Harry's vehicle.

It was unbelievable when I saw the car. The vehicle was apparently going down the street at a high rate of speed, and as he approached an intersection, he lost control. The vehicle did a couple of 360s and backed into the light pole. The vehicle exploded on contact with the pole and caught on fire. To describe what the vehicle looked like was almost impossible. The vehicle was traveling so fast that after he lost control, the vehicle backed into the light pole so quickly that there was a U shape indented into the trunk. The vehicle came to a rest with the pole up against the driver's seat. The impact was so great that they said Harry was killed instantly. The vehicle caught on fire, and his body was burned. When I looked at the steering wheel, it was bent into an oval shape, and you could see pieces of Harry's driving gloves burned to the steering wheel, along with skin from his fingers.

Harry had a closed casket funeral, and the guys from his shift were pallbearers. His wife was there, and when I looked at her, I do not think she handled it very badly. I wonder if she knew what Harry was going to do. He did not serve her the divorce papers yet, so instead of getting half, she got it all plus an insurance policy from the city and the state. I lost contact with her after the funeral and never saw her again. My wife didn't want to go to the funeral; I never asked her why.

Speed kills is what Roger said. But do we really know what happened? There were no witnesses to the accident. Some people say that when he approached the intersection, there may have been a car coming from his left; he tapped on his brakes and lost control. But if that was true, why didn't the car stick around? Was something bothering Harry? Did he have 100 percent of his mind and body on what he was doing? No one really knows. By the way, that fire that he was responding to was not a fire at all. The initial call was a gas station on fire. It turned out that the only thing on fire was an adding machine that had shorted out. He lost his life for an adding machine. That was a great trade, wasn't it?

Another officer, Joe, who worked midnights, was responding to a burglary at a pharmacy. He arrived, and his backup had not shown up yet. He pulled his vehicle up to the building and saw a second-floor window ajar. He got on the roof of his vehicle, and while attempting to pull himself up and into the opened window, the guy that was burglarizing the pharmacy put a .44-caliber barrel up to Joe's head and pulled the trigger. If you have never seen what a .44 caliber can do to something, you do not want to know. He couldn't wait for backup. This is the story I was told anyway. I was in the MP's when this happened. But there was a good thing that came out of it, if you want to call it that. There was a collection taken up for him, and enough money was collected to get us our first police dog. Yeah, that was a fair trade, wasn't it?

I didn't think it was a fair trade, but then late one shift, I and two other officers responded to a warehouse "burglary in progress" call. We surrounded the building, and then the K9 dog unit showed up. He made an announcement that they had a minute to come out or the dog was going in. Well, lo and behold, they said they would come out. They did and that was that.

One warm 28-degree February day, I was on routine patrol driving my favorite vehicle, number 1313. It was getting close to the end of my shift, and it was one of those days that there was not much to write to home about. I was sent on a call, and to this day, I don't remember what the call was. I turned into a strip mall parking lot to turn around and go back toward the direction I just came from. I saw this guy come out of a liquor store, look at me, and then go back inside. I thought to myself, *Either he forgot something or he was being very suspicious*. I called dispatch and advised them that I had a suspicious male at my location in the liquor store and requested backup. I gave them height, weight, race, and what he was wearing. He was a black male, twenty-five to twenty-eight years old, six feet and two inches, 225 pounds, wearing an Army fatigue jacket and blue jeans. Dispatch advised that no backup was available. I was on my own. I drove my vehicle up to about twenty-five feet from the front door so I could see the door and also the side door that was used for employees only.

While waiting for the guy to exit, a unit, an officer named Sid, came on the radio and said they would be my backup, but they were coming from the police station and their ETA (estimated time of arrival) was five minutes. Sid asked me what code he wanted me to have him respond. I told him that I was not sure what I had, but I did not feel right about this situation, so come on code 4. I then gave him a description of the guy. He said he would be there in about three minutes. Well, what I didn't know was when I asked for a code 4 response, a few other officers that were tied up on things dropped what they were doing and responded also.

It seemed like forever, but the guy walked out of the liquor store, looked at me, waved to me, and walked to his right toward the mall. I called for him; he looked and waved. I called again, and he waved. Finally, I was getting ready to get in my squad; he then stopped and walked toward me. I unsnapped my holster even though I did not know what I had going on. When the guy was within about eight to ten feet from me, I had him turn around and put his hands behind his head. I was going to do a stop and frisk search for weapons for *my* safety.

I started to search him with my left hand while my right hand was on my revolver. Just then, a gal came out of the employee's door on the right side of the building. He saw her also. He dropped his right hand and pulled a revolver from the front of his waist and turned toward me with a revolver in his hand. The split-second decision, which I still think about to this day, can I get my gun out in time? No, so I grabbed his wrist with my right hand, and we struggled for a second. He bent down, with me on his back, and fired one round. I felt it hit me under my bulletproof vest. He then said, "I'm going to kill you, you fucking pig." He stood up erect and fired one round over his left shoulder. That bullet felt like it hit me in my vest, but the impact knocked me to the ground. I then heard him discharge two more rounds.

As I was getting up off the parking lot, I saw him getting into my patrol car. I knelt down, drew my revolver, and fired five rounds into the door behind the driver. I fired a sixth round and took out the window behind the driver. All my firearms training at the range helped tremendously. I did the shooting instinctively as if it was second nature. I fired five rounds into the driver's rear door side in a four-inch circle and a sixth round into the rear door window. I reloaded and fired a seventh round at the rear window of the car just before he turned behind the liquor store. I was told later that the five rounds in the door were in a four inch circle at a 50 yard range. I carried my portable radio in the inside pocket of my jacket, so I reached for it and saw that the second bullet did not hit me in the vest; it went through my radio.

There was nothing I could do now but wait for backup. My stomach started to hurt really badly, and I thought to myself, *I've been shot*. Just then, an off-duty officer pulled up and witnessed the shooting and an officer going after the guy. I said, "No, the guy took my car." He stayed with me until help came. He kept telling me to lay down, but my gut hurt too much, like it was on fire; it felt better to just sit up.

The paramedics showed up, but because they thought that I hit my head, they couldn't give me anything for pain. They took off my shirt and vest and attended to my stomach wound. They also attended to the exit wound in my right buttocks. It looked to them like the bullet entered and exited. When I asked for something for pain, they continued to say no that if I hit my head and they gave me morphine, I could go into a coma. I had these real thin gloves that I wore on cold days. They were called search gloves, and they were soft and made from calf. I asked to put them into my mouth so I could bite on them. They complied.

The cops came like crazy that I could remember anyways. At this point, my mind was starting to go a little flaky. I was taken to the hospital about five blocks away. I had one IV in each arm and got one more in each arm when I got to the ER. They also were giving me blood in both carotid arteries since my arm veins were all used up. I remember about five officers that were there in the ER when Sergeant Russ came up and told me that they got him at a roadblock. Thanks to being a trained observer, I gave a very detailed description on radio when I requested a backup unit. He said the guy threw the gun away, and there were two police dogs looking for it. He asked me how many bullets the gun fired. I said four. A few minutes later, an officer came in and said that they had the gun. I said, "He fired four, right?" He said, "Yes, why?" I told him that I would tell him later. You see, when I was in basic training in the Army, they told us that you will never hear the bullet that kills you. It was very important to my well-being that the gun was found and to know that four bullets had been fired from it. Well, it was found and there were, so in my mind, I knew I was not going to die. Just then, a priest came up to me and was going to give me my last rights; being a nonpracticing Catholic, I knew what he was going to do. I looked at him and said, "Go away, Father. I am not going to die."

Just then, a doctor walked up to me and said, "Not doing too good, huh." I responded, "I hurt like hell." He looked at the paramedics and asked them if I had suffered a head wound, and they told him no. He then told the nurse to give me ten milligrams MS IV. That's ten milligrams of morphine. Apparently, I was borderline shocked, because I saw her put the need in the IV, start to push, but never saw her pull it out.

I woke up on day 4, filled with IVs, blood going into my neck, and a heart monitor keeping an eye on me. I was also on oxygen and had a tube going down my throat. I felt all the wires and tubes; I was going to strangle myself. The doctor came in and asked me how I was doing. I laughed and said okay. He told me that I had four sur-geries and eighteen pints of blood. I said that I thought we only had eight, and he told me that we did, but I was spitting it out as fast as they were putting it in. He also asked me if I knew that I had been shot twice. I said no. He told me that the first bullet went across my stomach and came within one layer of skin of exiting. He said he cut a hole in the right side of my stomach and pinched the skin like a pimple, and the bullet popped into his hand.

Then he had asked me what I had for lunch before I got shot. I told him that I had stopped home and had a couple of peanut-butter-and-jelly sandwiches. He laughed and said it was probably the peanut butter that had slowed the bullet down. He told me that he had to do a bowel resection, and I lost three and a half feet of intestines. He said he laid it down on the table and counted eigh-teen bullet holes. He then had to make an open incision below my waist on the left side to help fight infection. He would leave it open with a tube inserted so it could be cleaned out three times a day with hydrogen peroxide. He then told me that the exit wound in my buttocks was not an exit wound. The guy had shot me there also. Apparently, the bullet hit me in the right buttock, traveled through, made a perfect hole in my tailbone, and ended up in my left hip. I remember hearing two bullets when I was down, but he only hit me once—lucky me.

The days were kind of running together; my wife came and went. We did not talk much. Then some officers came in and took my statement. I gave it to them and still remember it today as if it was yesterday. My father always said, "The truth is easy to remember, but lies are hard to remember."

I started to have some problems with my intestines, so I had to go back to surgery to have a colostomy (a poop bag) put in for about four to six weeks; but I healed quickly, and they reversed it after three and a half weeks. I was back on the morphine, and let me tell you, that stuff is some mean shit. I had one night at about 2:00–3:00 a.m. and passed gas for the first time. The sound was so loud; it sounded like a gunshot, and I replayed the whole shooting again. But when it came time to pull my revolver, it wasn't there. I was scared to death.

There was another time on morphine when I started seeing little people walking on the steam pipe in my room. I had just watched the news, and the big story was "Who shot JR?" on the show *Dallas*. Well, I was asleep, heard a noise, and saw these characters from *Dallas* walking on the steam pipe, each one saying "I shot JR." Then JR walked out saying the same thing. They walked across the room on the pipe and exited the other wall. I was done with morphine; I hit the nurse button, and they put me on something else.

I got released to recoup and asked the doctor when I could go back to work. He said to give it some time and we would see. A few officers came to see me, but as time went by, there were less and less until they stopped visiting. Apparently, from what I could find out, officers felt vulnerable when they see an officer down. In order to cope with that, they stopped visiting.

After a few doctor visits, I asked him if I could bowl again, and he said to try it. I was bowling three to five leagues a week. I went bowling, and on my first ball, I fell down and could not figure out why.

Then again and again. It did not go well. On my next visit, I told my doctor, and he sent me to an orthopedic doctor. I went to see him; he did a CAT scan and said it looked like the bullet was in the hip joint. He recommended exploratory surgery, and I agreed.

When I woke up in my room, he was there; he said he dislocated the hip and found a piece of bullet that had shaved off in the joint before it ended up in the hip. He said he dug on my left hip joint for fifteen minutes and could not get the bullet out. So he popped the hip back in and stitched me up. He said if he couldn't get it out, Mother Nature sure wasn't going to pop it out.

After six weeks of physical therapy, I was released by all doctors to go back to work. I had been off work for nine long months with thirty-seven days in the hospital and five surgeries performed. I started the first week of October but was having problems exiting the vehicle. You see, when I got out and stood up, my left leg was still bent like I was sitting. I went to see Sergeant Boats, and he told me to put in for disability. I wasn't ready for that. I really loved my job.

I went to see workers' comp and told them that I wanted a second opinion. That doctor told me to retire. I said no. I asked the city to send me to a hip surgeon, and they said, "Who?"

I said, "An ortho for an NFL team."

They said, "Fine, pick a team."

I said, "Seattle was fine."

I flew to Seattle with the family and saw the doctor; he had me do tests and x-rays and then sat us down in his office a week later.

"What do you want to do in life?" he asked me.

"I want to be a cop." He then told me to find a new job.

We flew back. I told Sergeant Boats and put in for disability retirement. A week or so later, I saw the retirement doctor; and while he was looking over the doctor's report, he said, "You are retired."

Chapter 12

Time Alone or with...
(Don't Bring Your Spouse)

When Harry and I were still in the MPs together, he was starting to hang out with the city cops. He knew when he got out of the Army; he was going to the city. There was no career in the service for him. We were bowling one night, and while the wives were getting something to drink, he told me about a bar in the city. This was like any other kind of bar with one exception. If you were married, you could not bring your spouse there.

This was a special kind of bar; it was an "I want to vent" bar. Most of the guys that went to this bar were either by themselves or with someone else that was not their spouse. When I got in the city, I remembered the bar that Harry had talked about; and one night, I had to check it out.

I walked in and observed that it was your basic shot-and-a-beer bar. There were a few city guys there I recognized. I had no idea if the woman they were with were friends or worked on the force. The force was getting pretty big due to the expansion, and there were a lot of faces I didn't recognize.

I went and sat at the bar and listened to some of the conversations; they were interesting. But the subjects were split up between two categories from what I could hear: (1) they were talking about the day's activities, and (2) they were talking about how they could not talk to their wife about work.

I could not tell if there were any female officers there; I only knew two, and they were both married to officers. Policy was that they had to work separate shifts. Wow, that will keep a marriage together! Well, like I said, the topic of interest was my wife doesn't care. Even though I did not get involved in any of the conversations, I could see that these guys just needed to vent to someone. Maybe if their wives would've listened to them, they would've been home right now.

Remember when I talked about the kid that had committed suicide? Well, when I got home that night, for dinner, we were going to have spaghetti. All I could think of when I looked at the spaghetti was that little kid's brains all over the room. When my wife asked why I wasn't eating, I told her and she cut me off and said, "I don't want to hear about what happened at work today." A failure to communicate, I could see. So I kept my mouth shut, went and watched some TV, and then went to bed. The idea of seeing his brains with the combination of spaghetti and a noncommunicative marriage was really getting to me.

So here are these guys doing exactly what *I could not* do at home: communicate. It was like, well, you probably are not listening to me; but at the very least, I could vent to you. One thing I learned was that I was in the same boat with a bunch of other guys.

I do not know who the women were, but they were into the conversations. They may have worked in the records section, or they may have been dispatchers. I do not know because I never got to talk to them. They listened as the guys vented.

One conversation that I overheard was a dog handler who was talking about going into a warehouse. He said his dog got a scent on the bad guys, but the officer did not pick up the dog's signals. He was walking, and luckily, another officer found the guys before the dog handler. There is a lot of luck in an officer's day, like mine, when I got shot. If I had been early or late by two seconds, or even one, I would have missed being shot. That's what this officer was talking about: his luck. Well, today, it did not run out for him.

Most of the stories were about traffic stops or what the gal was wearing. "She was flirting with me," one officer discussed. "She even offered to give me her phone number if I did not write her a ticket. I did, and she didn't was how the story ended."

One guy was talking about a story where he was running radar. This guy driver and gal, who was pregnant, were speeding. The guy said he was speeding to get his pregnant wife to the hospital; she was having contractions. Well, the officer had a pregnant wife at home and felt sorry for the guy, so he gave him a police escort to the hospital. Because he decided to do this, he had to do a report. He was talking to the doctor, and the doctor said that the wife *was not* having contractions. The officer got so mad that even though there is no law against lying to a police officer, instead of giving the guy a speeding ticket, he gave him a ticket for negligent driving because he was endangering his unborn child and wife.

Now, I did not sense that this was the kind of bar that officers came to in order to cheat on their spouses. It was, like I said, an "I need to vent" bar. We had a psychologist on the force for guys to vent, but I do not know if anyone actually used that service. When Harry got killed, the department said anyone who wanted to see the counselor, could. If an officer was involved in a shooting, either him shooting someone or him getting shot, the psychologist was available. The department asked me if I wanted to see the psychologist after I got out of intensive care, and I said no. What can they do for me? They couldn't take the bullet away or give me a good hip. I did not think that mental counseling would help me.

What the department should've done was give the address of the bar to the psychologist and have him sit in these vent sessions. The officers would've been more at ease, and then maybe they would've been willing to talk. This is a very, very high-stress job. Your life, or someone else's, could be on the line at any call, at the drop of a hat. These guys needed to vent to somebody, and I guess that if the wife or spouse didn't want to listen, then they would find someone else who would.

Now, I never thought of this bar as a place for a guy to get a chick without the wife finding out. I really believed it to be a "venting" bar. I could see why a guy should not bring his spouse. If I was talking to a gal at a table and one of her friends came in and saw me, it would have been over sooner. My wife and I split about one year after I took my disability retirement.

So is an officer, who is married to a spouse that won't listen, wrong to vent to someone else? I do not think so. Is the officer wrong if he wants to vent to someone other than his spouse while in bed with that someone else? Yes, of course.

Chapter 13

If You Aren't, Don't; if You Are, Communicate

Now that I have scared you about being a police officer, let me throw some facts at you. The law firm in England of Hartnell Chanot and Partners advises that the rate of police divorces is two times the national average. Let me say that again, *two times* the national average of England. If you google[4] divorces, there is a study that was done; and while interviewing spouses, 75 percent say that they have been divorced at least once. When I took my disability from my shooting, I was working as a retail manager. I was helping a gal who was shopping for her husband that was the chief of police in a town west of where I was working. She told me that she was wife number eight, and to quote her, "I *will* be his last one." That was about twelve years ago; he's probably had about four or five more wives since then.

So you ask, why did I write all these gory stories in the other chapters? Well, it was not to scare you. If you want to be a cop, fine. That isn't why I wrote this book. I am telling you that, sure, be a cop, but do not, I repeat, *do not*, get married, unless you do a bunch of things together before you get married. Let us start with the basics: "Honey, I want to become a police officer. What do you think?"

---

4   Google.com.

Listen to your spouse. What are the negatives of being a cop? Let's see—overtime, the pay, not being home, the chance of getting killed. Now, everyone is going to die, unless they find the fountain of youth; but being a cop, you could be killed any day of the week.

Here are more statistics you need to consider: (1) a divorce rate that is 60–70 percent higher than the national average, (2) an alcoholism rate that is two times the national average, (3) a domestic violence rate that is among the highest of all professions, and (4) suicide rate that is three times the national average. These statistics come from the Police Dynamics Institute.[5]

Again, I am *not* telling you to not go into law enforcement; I am telling you not to take a spouse with you unless you do a bunch of things together to research this new career. This is not like being a doctor or an attorney where you are gone most of the day. This is a job that not only puts stress on you at work, but if there is no communication at the home, there will be more stress.

Is all the stress necessary? Do you want to go on your first call of the day with an argument you and your spouse had at breakfast over you working too much? Or was it "You come home and go straight to bed" or "You don't come home right after work because you have to hang out with the guys for a few hours"?

These are the things I am talking about. If you are not married and become a police officer, that is one thing. But if you are married, there is a *family* that is now in law enforcement. If you are single and you find a prospective mate and they have the hots for you, set them straight: "This is what I do…"

Now, sure, you are going to say, "Oh, my marriage will be different." Yeah, right, everybody says that. Then they get divorced. I know that when you use the word average, it is just that: an average. You go to work for the start of your shift, and you count twenty officers; 75 percent have been divorced or will be. That's roughly fifteen officers on the shift.

Here is what you can do. If you are married and the person is so goo-goo-eyed over you that they won't listen, have the talk with

---

5   Police Dynamics Institute, Summerville, SC.

other spouses. Find out what pressures the other spouse is under. And make sure they tell the truth. In my tenure as a police officer, I think I met maybe three spouses that were able to live with it, and I think it helped that they did not have any kids, which brings me to another subject—kids. My dad/mom is a police officer, but I never see them because they are always working. I don't even want to go there because it could be another book by itself.

So okay, either you are already married or you are going to get married while being a police officer. Go talk to the police chaplain (if the force has one) or the police psychologist/psychiatrist. You and the spouse or future spouse should sit down with this person and ask questions. Are there a lot of problems in a police family? If so, what are those problems?

If this book gets published, read it and read it again. When you are done, give it to your mate (I say mate because I don't want to say wife because there are also female officers with husbands or boyfriends), and let them read it. Let them see what you are going through. See if they want to go through the "silence at home" after you respond to a SIDS death or a juvenile suicide. You cannot have a spouse that says "Leave your job at the front door." They have to be considerate of your emotions, and there will be some.

After I started on the force and had no "shoulder to cry on," so to speak, I became very cold. I looked at things in a black-and-white state. I learned to laugh things off. Some people said that I had a sick sense of humor. I told them it was either that or alcoholism. My problem of no emotions carried on past my police disability and affected my marriage and my relationships with my children. Will I ever get over it? I do not know. Maybe after my shooting when the police offered me "shrink services," I should have taken them instead of saying "I'm fine."

So you get to the process and find out if there is a meeting with the department psychologist that involves you and the spouse or mate. Remember we are talking a very high divorce rate. Would you not want them to sit in? Oh, yeah, it's not going to happen to you—divorce, right? Yeah, okay.

Find out if the force has a weekly or monthly rap session with officers and spouses, and if they do not, find out why not. As high as the divorce rate is, you would think the department would want to get involved. You must learn to open up to someone. I do not care if it is to the department, the wife, girlfriend/boyfriend, husband, or whoever. Just don't open up to your girl/boy if you are married because then you are now past the point of no return. Find the problem before it gets to that.

A relative of mine came up to me and told me that they were considering becoming a police officer. They asked me what I thought. I said, "Great, just don't get married. Stay single." That is where the "dedication" came from. The title of this book, *The Silent Badge*, has two meanings. Hopefully, you have figured them out by now. If you still haven't, they are these: do not stay silent at home because your problems at home could cause you to lose your edge at work, and then you will become the silent badge.

Good luck in your decision of becoming a police officer. Always sit with your back to a wall, and always kiss your spouse and children and tell them how great it is to be home.

Chapter 14

The End: The Speech

While growing up, I never thought about being a police officer. In fact, I wanted to be a history teacher. My parents wanted me to be a vet because I always had a thing with animals. Well, fate brought me to the crossroads of being a police officer, and I would not have changed one thing even the part when I "bought a couple."

Well, so it happened. I have told you a lot; there will not be a test but, instead, a speech. I am going to summarize this book into a few sentences.

It takes a special person, a special breed, to become a police officer. If you are married or going to get married, make sure you communicate. Make sure this is what you want to do. You need to learn to use your brain. Police officers are smart people. They have to go through a lot to get on the road.

Once you and your spouse have come to the decision you are going to do it, throw prejudice out the window. If you are white and don't like blacks, don't become a cop. If you are black and don't like whites, don't become a cop. It will come back some day to bite you in the ass. The same goes unsaid about any other race you may not like.

Just because you have a gun doesn't mean you get to shoot people. You are there to protect lives and property. Sometimes, talking will do just fine. So grow some balls. Females can have them too.

Show respect to others. Once a year, I go to a police retirement get-together. We have come to the conclusion that we are glad we are retired and not on the street today. Back then, if we told someone to stop (with a few exceptions), they stopped. Today, they run. There is no respect for the law, and in turn, there is no respect for John Doe citizen. Years ago, there was a bumper sticker that read "If you don't like cops and need help, call a hippie." Why don't people like cops? This is important if you are going to be one.

If you cannot handle blood, guts, or dead people, find a different career. If you cannot talk to your spouse today, do you think you will be able to talk to them later when you become a police officer? Probably not.

Whenever I had a class in school, the teacher would say, "Okay, this will be on the test; remember this." Then they would tell us something.

So, Okay, this is on the test. Remember this… Talk to your spouse and family, don't be prejudice, and use your brain. Get very, very good with your firearm. The life you save may be your own or someone else's loved one. I don't want to hear or read in the news that officers fired 50 rounds and hit a suspect twice. While I was on the force, I hit the range for 50 rounds a month and had to qualify once a quarter. As police officers we are charged to protect and serve. Our jobs can be frustrating because there are times when those we work to Protect and Serve do not respect our role or true commitment to our communities. This is our lot in life, but we will continue to Protect and Serve. My hope is that our communities will understand that the majority of us are truly committed to this mission and will support us each and every day as we risk our lives to protect them. Lastly, I will remind you of what my father told me many years ago… "what awaits you will never miss you." After many years of battling with surgeries necessary to fix my initial shooting injuries, I have found peace with all of it and want to share this with my fellow officers of the law. At the age of 60, I found my soulmate and I have regained peace about my past. May all of you continue to Protect, Serve and Be Safe.

Amen.

About the Author

Photo by
Kelly Manteck - KAMera Photo

Born and raised in the southwest (Westmont, Brookfield, and Lyons) area of Chicago, Steven F. Verzal was raised in a close and large blue-collar family. At the age of eighteen, he enlisted in the US Army, ready to defend his country. The Army opted to move him from the infantry to the military police in Anchorage, Alaska, at Fort Richardson. It was then that he knew the police work was his calling. After serving in the Army for six years, Steven was recruited and joined the Anchorage Police Department. During his career at APD, Officer Verzal was critically wounded during an armed robbery at a liquor store. After nine months of recovery from multiple gunshot wounds, Officer Verzal was forced to take a disability retirement due to the sustained injuries and the remaining bullet that was lodged in his hip. To this day, Officer Verzal considers his jobs in law enforcement his "favorite" job and only has regrets that he could not continue that career path. Steven currently resides in Las Vegas, Nevada, with his wife, Nancy. Steven started writing this book many years ago. After much introspection, Steven opted to complete this work in hopes of assisting other first responders about the highs, lows, and hindsight advice for this career path. Steven, finding his new calling, has started writing a murder mystery series, starring Sam, the Alaskan and his quirky partner, Ed.

CPSIA information can be obtained
at www.ICGtesting.com
Printed in the USA
BVHW081050191119
564175BV00009B/780/P